W9-BAR-894

Corporate Governance
and Risk

Corporate Governance and Risk

A Systems Approach

JOHN C. SHAW

WILEY

John Wiley & Sons, Inc.

For general information on our other products and services, or technical support, please contact our Customer Care Department within the United States at 800-762-2974, outside the United States at 317-572-3993 or fax 317-572-4002.

Wiley also publishes its books in a variety of electronic formats. Some content that appears in print may not be available in electronic books.

For more information about Wiley products, visit our web site at www.wiley.com.

Designations used by companies to distinguish their products are often claimed by trademarks. In all instances where the author or publisher is aware of a claim, the product names appear in Initial Capital letters. Readers, however, should contact the appropriate companies for more complete information regarding trademarks and registration.

Library of Congress Cataloging-in-Publication Data:

Shaw, J. C. (John Calman), 1932–
    Corporate governance and risk : a systems approach / John C. Shaw.
        p.   cm.—(Wiley finance series)
    Includes bibliographical references.
        ISBN 0-471-44547-9
        1. Corporate governance.   2. Risk management.   I. Title.   II. Series.
    HD2741.5485   2003
    658.15'5—dc21   2003003964

Printed in the United States of America.

10   9   8   7   6   5   4   3   2   1

Other Books
by John C. Shaw

Managing Computer Systems Projects
(with William Atkins), McGraw-Hill, 1970.

Managing the EDP Function (with Arnold E. Ditri
and William Atkins), McGraw-Hill, 1971.

*The Quality-Productivity Connection in
Service-Sector Management*, Van Nostrand Reinhold, 1978.

*The Service Focus—Developing Winning Game
Plans for Service Companies*, Dow Jones–Irwin, 1990.

Acknowledgments

This book is based in large part on the risk management and corporate governance work of one of the nation's leading professional services firms, Deloitte & Touche, and in particular, its Enterprise Risk Services (ERS) practice. As part of its ongoing effort to help clients manage risk and uncertainty throughout the enterprise, ERS' global leader, Bob Rothermel, invited me to work with a group of my former colleagues at Deloitte & Touche to develop a thought-provoking document that demonstrated their unique point of view. He and the firm have further agreed to allow me to use some of the concepts developed as part of that project in this book, in particular those based on Systems Thinking.

Many people have provided invaluable input to both that project and this book, in particular the group of Deloitte & Touche professionals whose names are listed here in alphabetical order. While the firm has graciously permitted me to use many of the ideas we developed in our work together, the concepts remain the property of Deloitte & Touche. Nevertheless, the responsibility for the accuracy, readability, and comprehensiveness of this text rests solely with me.

My special thanks to Bob Rothermel, who was the driving force behind the Deloitte & Touche project in which I had the pleasure to be involved. Without him that project would not have been the success it was and I would not be in the position to share this work with you.

DELOITTE & TOUCHE
CONTRIBUTORS AND REVIEWERS

Tom Church
Cathi Cunningham
Bill Foote
Rick Funston
Ami Kaplan
Mark Layton
Chris Mitchell
Bob Rothermel
Bob Walsh

My Deloitte & Touche colleagues made other, behind-the-scenes contributions to this work as well:

Myles Currie
Steve Doyle
Jane Longfellow
Mary Ann McMahon
Andy Shomph
Diane Smrekar

Without them, the logic, editing, and production of this work could not have taken place.

In addition to my Deloitte & Touche colleagues, I owe an enormous debt of gratitude to my wife, Ellen Shockro. Ellen provided the motivation, inspiration, leadership, and patience necessary to see a project such as this from start to finish.

I have acknowledged many of those who contributed directly to this book in the text itself; however, there are others who have made important contributions that have made this project possible, including:

John L. Carl, former Senior Vice President, Chief Financial Officer, Allstate Insurance Company.
James M. Denny, Vice Chairman, Retired, Sears, Roebuck & Co.
Jeanne Glasser, Senior Editor, John Wiley & Sons, Inc.
Fred Goldwater, Senior Vice President, Blue Cross Blue Shield North Carolina.
Martha Clark Goss, former Senior Vice President, Prudential Insurance Company of America; Independent Board Member.
Frances Hesselbien, Chairman, Leader to Leader Foundation.
Nan Stone, Partner, Bridgespan Group; Former Editor, *Harvard Business Review*.
Douglas West, Senior Vice President, Government and Industry Affairs, Toyota Motors, North America.

In addition, I wish to express my appreciation for the commitment of Physicians Mutual Insurance Company in Omaha and their senior executives including:

Robert Reed, President and CEO.
Ed Graycar, Executive Vice President and COO.
Roger Hermsen, Executive Vice President and CFO.
Gene Theel, Executive Vice President.

Rob Reed, Senior Vice President, Direct Marketing.
Larry Beldin, Senior Vice President, Corporate Services.
Ed Horwitz, Senior Vice President, Market Segment Officer.
Don Van Scyoc, Senior Vice President, Market Segment Officer.

Physicians Mutual provided valuable feedback and learning that contributed enormously to this project.

Contents

The book you're about to read provides an innovative approach to thinking about the future of governance and risk.

Today, we work in an uncertain world that's both volatile and complex. Through *Corporate Governance and Risk: A Systems Approach*, John C. Shaw, a retired senior consulting partner and vice chairman of our firm, together with my colleagues in the Enterprise Risk Services practice of Deloitte & Touche, present a new and useful framework for making critical business decisions across the enterprise. I know their approach will help senior executives and their boards of directors develop new options, consider consequences—including those that may be unintended—and understand the potential risks and rewards of the decisions they make.

Perhaps more importantly, this work provides definition and clarity around the real issues of governance and risk. Indeed, the thesis of this work defines governance, not from the narrow focus of regulatory compliance, but from the perspective of decision making. Enterprise risks and rewards then become the potential outcomes of the choices available and the decisions taken by boards and senior executives.

Why is this important? Your organization's ability to make the right decisions is integral to creating competitive advantage. *Corporate Governance and Risk* provides a template for anticipating, understanding, and taking action around the consequences of choices and decisions. Using this blueprint can help you build competitive advantage, while helping to insulate your enterprise from the abuses, excesses, and ethical lapses that have dominated recent headlines.

In a business environment that routinely functions at the speed of light, you need every legitimate advantage you can muster. Today, instantaneous communications pulsing across global networks enable us to gather and sort amazing amounts of information. I've experienced this firsthand. As the chief executive officer of a global organization, I led the dramatic shift from a world of loosely affiliated national firms to a more integrated structure whose member firms are capable of better providing seamless, high-quality service to any client regardless of geography. However, our technology far outpaced our decision making capabilities. We still needed effective processes for the decision making required to help us lead our business forward. Looking back, I know now that *Corporate Governance and Risk* would have served as a superb resource to help guide my thinking in this area.

You should consider this book as one of the most important tools you can use to craft better and more effective decisions. *Corporate Governance and Risk* provides a framework, process, and body of knowledge specifically designed to help boards, executive management, and makers of public policy and regulation anticipate, understand, and take action around the consequences of their choices and decisions—and take responsibility for those outcomes. Hopefully, this work will serve as a stimulus for thinking about governance and risk in very different ways.

You'll find that one of the book's best features is its ability to help you visualize beyond the horizon. As you know, boards and executive management are both accountable and responsible for the outcomes of their decisions—now, and *in the future*. This is a critical point. We've all seen the results of what Jack Shaw calls "Big Decisions" occur at different places and times. When those results make themselves known many months or years after the original decision has been made—as is possible with Big Decisions of public policy and regulation—they can carry unintended consequences far removed from those envisioned when the original decision was made.

Jack Shaw and my colleagues have written a book for the future that is here for you today. We're at the dawn of an exciting new era—one in which governance will become synonymous with decision making, and risk will often be exceeded by the potential for reward. *Corporate Governance and Risk* is a book that has anticipated the new challenges of our times, and shares with us an approach to help you and your business dictate events, rather than be overcome by them.

I urge you to read this book.

By using its many insights and applying its lessons every day, you'll take a significant step toward reaping the rewards of tomorrow.

JAMES E. COPELAND, JR.
Former Chief Executive Officer
Deloitte & Touch LLP
Deloitte Touche Tohmatsu

February 2003

Preface

As you will soon see, this book is milestone 17 in a journey of discovery around the subject of governance and risk. I wrote this Preface after I had written and organized the chapters in order to provide the reader with a road map through the logical framework of the book. I am very hopeful that this section will be of help to the reader in really using and benefiting from this book.

My intention and purpose in writing this book is to provide board members and other chief or "C-level" executives with an additional point of view or perspective on the companion subjects of governance and risk. At the end of 2002 a great deal has been written and many seminars conducted on the subject of governance, in particular, following the passage of the Sarbanes-Oxley Act of 2002.

This book is not about Sarbanes-Oxley or any other legal or regulatory aspect of corporate governance. While the provisions of Sarbanes-Oxley are cited and referred to throughout the book, they are highlighted in the context of the framework and process that is really the subject of the book. Rather, this book is designed to provide a structure within which the reader may place the many and varied topics being introduced under the subjects of governance and risk. Said another way, this is not a recipe-driven cookbook, but a book on how to cook.

Speaking of subjects, the chapter endnotes provide the reader with further background into the various publications I found useful during the course of researching and organizing this book. The materials I have made reference to encompass subjects that may seem far afield from those of governance and risk; however, this book is the result of a far-ranging journey into the myriad of topics which, at least in my mind, have come together into a framework and process.

I specifically focused the structure and content of this book as a top-down, high-level guide to assist board members and other chief or C-level executives to better understand and perform their roles in this complex, volatile, and stressful time. I am introducing a framework for thinking about governance and risk and a process for implementation. The chapters of this book are designed to make the case for a different perspective and then to take the reader through the detailed steps required to understand and act upon what needs to be done in order for organizations to be more effective in this new world of governance and risk. At this point, the reader may find it helpful to skip ahead and preview Chapter 10, "Making It Happen," to gain at least my perspective on making change. Following is a chapter-by-chapter guide through the book.

CHAPTER 1   THE JOURNEY

As the title implies, this chapter is a description of the major milestones in the 17-year journey of discovery of the elusive and multiple dimensions of the subjects of governance and risk. Like most journeys, this one had dead ends and wrong turns, and provided tremendous learning. The journey served many purposes, but perhaps the most important discovery was the need to narrow down the definitions and myriad points of view. I really believe that definition and focus are necessary if learning is to take place and if this book is to be more than a catalog of different points of view. The Lessons Learned section of this chapter provides the base on which the rest of the book is built.

CHAPTER 2   A CURRENT PERSPECTIVE: WHY THINGS GO WRONG

At a very high and conceptual level, this chapter deals with the two reasons that I have discovered which explain why things don't turn out the way we generally think they should or will. The first reason is what I call conventional wisdom about *what* constitutes the combined subjects of governance and risk according to most parties. The second reason is *how* we are organized within most enterprises, a state I call fragmentation, for dealing with both subjects. In effect, this chapter is intended to define the problem that the book is designed to address.

CHAPTER 3   CHANGING THE PERSPECTIVE: WHY THINGS REALLY HAPPEN THE WAY THEY DO

Again, at a high and conceptual level, this chapter provides a scientific basis for designing the framework and process required to establish a new perspective on the subjects of governance and risk. This chapter introduces the concept of Systems Thinking. This concept provides the basis for the Governance Model and the System of Governance, which are the forces of this book.

CHAPTER 4   THE EXTENDED ENTERPRISE: WE ARE ALL CONNECTED

This subject of the Extended Enterprise is introduced early in this book to provide the reader with a perspective on the organization that goes far beyond the legal boundaries of the firm. Not only do we live in a networked world, but we also conduct our business with players, many of whom we do not know, who perform a large number of the value-added activities of our enterprise but who also expose us to previously unknown risks.

CHAPTER 5   THE GOVERNANCE MODEL AND THE SYSTEM OF GOVERNANCE

This chapter outlines the overall structure of both the Governance, Model and the System of Governance, which were introduced in Chapter 3. This chapter first considers the whole of both the Governance Model and the System of Governance, which deal with the *what* of risk and the *how* of governance prior to introducing the details of each system. This chapter provides the reader with high-level examples of choices and decisions together with related outcomes or consequences of those choices and decisions. This chapter also introduces a structure that will be used throughout the remaining chapters:

■ Big Decisions
■ Management

Big Decisions identify, for each subsystem of the Governance Model, the nature of the decisions generally experienced at that level. It is my hope that the reader may use Big Decisions as a basis for relating specifically to the choices and decisions facing his or her own organization. Management is further broken down within each subsystem of the Governance Model:

■ Roles of those having the greatest decision-making accountability and responsibility.
■ Processes/activities that are often found within a particular level of decision making.
■ Methodologies available, including tools and techniques used to facilitate decision making.

CHAPTER 6   STRATEGY—OUTCOMES ASSOCIATED WITH THE FUTURE

Strategy is the first of the major subsystems of the Governance Model. From a governance and risk standpoint, strategy deals with the first and highest levels of uncertainty. The Governance Model introduces ways for the board and senior executives to consider the unknown and perhaps unknowable.

CHAPTER 7   EXECUTION—OUTCOMES THAT ARE, OR SHOULD BE, KNOWABLE

Execution means, what we do to implement the strategies designed to enable the enterprise to survive and grow, and what are the intended and unintended consequences of the strategy and the means of execution. Execution is a continuation of the process for implementing the Governance Model and the System of Governance.

CHAPTER 8   OPERATIONS—OUTCOMES ASSOCIATED WITH THE PRESENT

Operations is a continuation of the Governance Model, which works through strategy to execution to operations. Operations converts the long-term, perhaps unknowable aspects of strategy to the shorter-term, knowable issues of execution to the details of the coming year, which, with detail planning, should be quite certain.

CHAPTER 9   ORGANIZATION, MANAGEMENT PROCESS, AND INFORMATION

This chapter provides the structure, processes, and information that hold the Governance Model and the System of Governance together. Issues of who does what and how information provides the fact base required for effective decision making are the topics of this chapter. In particular, the role of the governance committee of the board as well as the roles of the major decision-making bodies of the enterprise are highlighted.

CHAPTER 10   MAKING IT HAPPEN

You will see that I have used the Governance Model and System of Governance as the framework or subject matter of implementation. In other words, I have designed an implementation process that uses the framework to bootstrap or load itself under two models of change, transitional and transformational. Each model of change is actually implemented through a three-phase process with a "Plan to Plan" included illustrating the details of each phase.

CHAPTER 11   WHERE DO WE GO FROM HERE? THOUGHTS FOR THE BOARD AND CHIEF OR C-LEVEL EXECUTIVES

This chapter is intended to provide personal guidance and direction to the intended audience of this book. I have tried to put myself in your shoes and to provide you with a perspective on your roles that, while I am sure most of you have considered the subject, brings back the basic messages as to who is accountable for what and why the acceptance of responsibilities as decision makers, including the consequences of those decisions, is your job.

You now see the scope of the journey you are to take. Hopefully, it will be a journey of learning. It will not be a bottom-up journey of checklists and dos and do-nots. My whole approach to this book was to provide a framework and process that you could apply to the various roles you play within the enterprise. I look forward to hearing from you and learning as I move to my next milestones.

JOHN C. SHAW

Stonington, Deer Isle, Maine
February 2003

Risk is a choice rather than a fate. The actions we dare to take, which depend on how free we are to make choices, are what the story of risk is all about. And that story helps define what it means to be a human being.

—*Against the Gods, The Remarkable Story of Risk*,
Peter L. Bernstein (John Wiley & Sons, Inc., 1996)

PART
One

Establishing a
Perspective

CHAPTER 1

The Journey

INTRODUCTION

My journey began 17 years ago and has now reached a point where it seems appropriate to stop, take a deep breath, look around, and consolidate my learning. In view of our turbulent and volatile times, there will undoubtedly be more learnings; however, at this point I believe I have gained enough experience to put forth what I believe to be a different perspective on the twin subjects of governance and risk.

Milestone 17

This book is an intermediate milestone that I call Milestone 17 in an endless journey of self-discovery. I have an insatiable appetite for new ideas, concepts, and learning and in particular seek to gain a better understanding of *why* things work or don't work as we think they should.

For example, during the 17-year journey of discovery around the subject of risk, it never ceased to amaze me that we were constantly surprised when things did not turn out the way we thought they would. After examining the bodies of knowledge available on other business subjects such as finance and accounting, marketing, information technology, and human resource management, I felt there was something to be learned, taught, tested, and made to work. As Peter Drucker has shown us, even nebulous subjects such as management and leadership may be codified and employed with great success.

However, notwithstanding all of the research and financial resources devoted to risk, there is no complete body of knowledge that defines risk, except in the narrowest sense. There is no body of knowledge that describes the management of risk in terms one could point to as workable.

The 17-year journey has reached a point at which I feel that I have learned enough to go public with a framework for thinking about governance and risk as well as a workable process for implementation. I think that the frameworks and processes for thinking about governance and risk are sufficiently grounded in both the physical and social sciences that they may be trusted to produce promised outcomes, that is, an explanation of *why* things work or don't work as we think they should.

A final point before launching into the milestones that have passed before reaching Milestone 17, a single unanswered question has been in the back of my mind throughout the journey:

> *Is there a difference between good management and the management of risk?*

The answer to my rhetorical question has two parts. First, there is a body of knowledge around what Peter Drucker calls the practice of management.[1] Essentially that body of knowledge focuses the enterprise on an inside-out customer perspective and on the value of the human resource; and second, *I do not believe the traditional ways of managing risk are any longer sufficient. Our thinking has progressed, and we now need to take risk management to a new level. Good management and the management of risk are two different concepts.*

This book will support the second part of the answer and provide a framework and process for implementing what I have come to call the Governance Model.

A Failure in 1985 Started the Trip

I began this journey of studying and attempting to understand risk at the request of a long-standing client. The CEO of a large financial services company asked me to undertake a study of what might go wrong, that is, what might be the risks associated with a recent acquisition (an interesting question to be asking after the decision was made and the transaction closed). My colleagues and I undertook the task of developing a framework for assessing risks in what I will call a static fashion—that is, what sorts of risks might be detected at any point in time. The framework we developed was quite elaborate; the client was satisfied; and with the permission of the client, I went on to describe the approach to many and varied audiences.

At the point in time the work was completed we may have understood some of the potential risks and categories of risk, but in the dynamic world of financial services our view was obsolete by the next day. Four years later, both the parent and the subsidiary had nearly failed; management was replaced; and a public relations nightmare ensued. As you can imagine, that experience taught me a lot about what risk management was not, but little about what risk management was. My journey had started. At that point, I chalked up the near failure of the client as a failure of implementation. I was right and wrong!

This book has had many authors as the journey of discovery progressed. I will continue to acknowledge those who influenced my thinking as we move through time. I will also begin to convey the learning that took place in a section of this chapter called Lessons Learned. It was and is those lessons learned that formed the need and basis for this book.

During the course of my journey over the past 17 years, I have conducted scores of interviews, visited many companies, and digested as much of the current literature on risk as I could find. The chapter endnotes sections identify those readings that I found particularly useful.

This book is heavily grounded in the research that I conducted on my own as well as with my colleagues at Deloitte & Touche LLP. In the interest of ease of readability, I chose not to insert references in the main body of the text in the form of quotations and footnotes. Rather, I took the liberty of interpreting and applying the research and references as examples, illustrations, or cases. Throughout my journey of discovery, I was continuously reminded of the client's near failure related earlier as well as a deep desire to try to understand why things happen or don't happen the way they should. The real test of the ideas put forth in this book will be whether they will be as relevant to future decision making as they are, with hindsight, to past decisions. In my efforts to look to the future, you will see the following phrase appear many times throughout this book: *anticipate, understand, and take action* around the choices available, the intended and unintended consequences of the decisions made from among those choices, and the feedback and learning that take place.

As a final introductory point, before proceeding further you may wish to read Chapter 10, "Making It Happen," which presents strategies for implementation. Think about the nature of your organization in terms of the requirements for change. Consider if your organization may be a candidate for transitional change whereby you simply improve something that is already great or whether the organization must transform itself. With the model of change in mind, continue your journey through this book.

THE MILESTONES

My journey has been, and will continue to be, one of research of current and historical literature; interviews with knowledgeable people; analysis of long-term shareowner value creation; as well as a journey of self-discovery. This book, and the follow-on feedback and learning that I expect to receive from readers, will enrich my experiences and continue to build a body of knowledge on the subject of governance and risk. The following is an interim time line of milestones passed so far in this journey, and the learnings from which I formed the basis for this book:

1985–1991
- The development of a risk assessment framework and process that did not work over the long run.
- Continued refinement and challenge of ideas.
- The proliferation of organizations, books, and research.

1992–2000
- Introduction to the concepts of General Systems Theory and Systems Thinking.
- Work with Peter Drucker.
- Deloitte & Touche Enterprise Risk Services task force.
- "Irrational exuberance"—the dot-com boom and the new economy.
- Y2K—the day nothing happened!
- March 2000—the beginning of the end, or the end of the beginning?

2001 Onward
- September 11, 2001—the ultimate crisis.
- The scandals.
- Three models.
- The uncertainty.

The following paragraphs briefly summarize the learnings at each milestone and the impact those learnings have had on the issues of governance and risk.

1985–1991

The 1985–1991 portion of my journey was, at once, my least productive and my most productive segment. I learned what did not work, or what worked only temporarily, in terms of my understanding of why outcomes did not come about as originally planned. I also learned that others researching the subject of risk had not arrived at solutions that were any better than mine.

Development of a Risk Assessment Framework and Process That Did Not Work

It may seem strange to cite a failure as a basis for learning; however, my passion to achieve an ever-deepening understanding of *why* has shaped much of my professional career. We all learn something from our mistakes, however; I do think we learn more from the feedback that characterizes our successes. The development of the risk assessment framework of 1985 was not a failure at the time in the eyes of my client or my colleagues. Like much of what I will describe as Systems Thinking in later chapters, the solution to the problem we addressed in 1985 led to unintended consequences that surfaced in 1989. Neither the risk assessment framework nor the process for implementation prevented the problems of governance and risk that nearly brought down the parent and its subsidiary in 1992 and beyond. Here is why:

- The risk assessment framework, although very broad in scope, focused on outcomes—the results of decisions as opposed to the decisions themselves. The potential outcomes or consequences of decisions are not only nearly infinite in number, but they are also dependent on the time frames of uncertainty. The framework could deal only with a static view—*today*.
- The framework attempted to combine both the risk-bearing nature of the products of a financial services company and the business of being a financial services company. One framework cannot handle both. The decisions and processes are too different to be integrated into one framework. This book will deal with the decision-making processes around the enterprise and its environment, but will only refer to those aspects of the Governance Model and the process for implementation that deal with the products of the enterprise.
- The process of implementation was not considered as an integral part of the framework itself. The risk assessment framework cannot implement itself, and the issues of transitional or transformational change management were not adequately considered.
- The framework considered risk across the enterprise but did not explicitly consider the ideas of cause and effect, feedback and learning, which would prove to be so important to the real problems of governance and risk.

Finally, the framework did not deal with the organization's values or culture—issues that my colleague Martha Clark Goss has described as "tone at the top." Martha, a longtime client and friend of Deloitte & Touche, has studied and specialized in the issues of culture and governance. I will cite her work throughout this book as being extremely important to the culture and *behavior* of everyone from board members through transaction processors.

Continued Refinement and Challenge of Ideas

The final years of the 1980s led to my continuing journey and search for a unifying theory around why some enterprises are successful through good times and bad and why some organizations recover from crises of one kind or another while most do not. I worked with some organizations with familiar household names and others that could be characterized as mom-and-pop start-ups or closely held family businesses. I wrote a book and taught strategy at Stanford and Wharton in an effort to put more discipline into my thinking. I led a number of turnaround and strategy projects as a consultant and ran numerous client and association seminars on strategy and risk. I learned a lot, but achieved no breakthroughs.

Proliferation of Organizations, Books, and Research

During this quest for a way of explaining long-term success and failure beyond the traditional work of consulting firms and business schools, I collected everything I could get my hands on, including:

- *Keeping Good Company: A Study of Corporate Governance in Five Countries*, by Jonathan Charkham (New York: Oxford University Press, 1994).
- "Mastering Risk," a 10-part series by the *Financial Times* (London: Financial Times Limited, 2000).
- National Association of Corporate Directors' Report of the NACD Blue Ribbon Commission on Director Professionalism, 1996.
- Securities and Exchange Commission (SEC) Regulation Fair Disclosure, October 2000.
- Committee of Sponsoring Organizations (COSO) of the Treadway Commission, Internal Control Integrated Framework, 1992.

I spent a great deal of time looking for common themes or insights that would tie things together into a picture or framework from which I could establish a hypothesis and conduct research. What I encountered was a number of tools and techniques without a toolbox to hold them together. Each of the tools I examined from all sources was useful in its own right, but there was no unifying concept among or between the most detailed concepts of governance and risk. I needed a framework—a toolbox—and there was not one available other than the one I had worked on in 1985.

1992–2000

In my pursuit of lifetime learning and to deal with my passion around a deeper understanding and a framework for understanding why things happen the way they do, I enrolled in the doctoral program at Claremont Graduate University in Claremont, California. I felt that the discipline of formal research—particularly on the question of why, despite nearly 100 years of the development of the practice of management, things generally don't turn out the way we think they will—would help me in my own consulting practice and my thoughts about the subject of risk.

Introduction to Concepts of General Systems Theory and Systems Thinking

Most of us almost intuitively grasp the idea of cause and effect and issues of intended and unintended consequences. As professionals and as managers, we all have asked the questions:

- What makes you think this will work?
- What new problems will this solution create?
- What happens next?
- Is the medicine worse than the disease?

In my experience, the more rigorously we ask these questions, the less risk we run of what I call "solving the wrong problem."

Further, only recently have the social sciences of philosophy, psychology, economics, and sociology become entwined with the physical sciences of mathematics, physics, and chemistry.

As we will see later, with the exception of Peter Drucker's contribution, the physical sciences dominated management thinking for the entire twentieth century.

The integration of the physical and social sciences led the way to a new way of thinking about why things work the way they do and why, despite our best intentions, there are always unintended consequences. General Systems Theory and Systems Thinking were topics that really interested me at Claremont because they began to explain, for me, why things work or don't work as they are intended. A framework for thinking about risk was beginning to emerge.

Of course, different ways of thinking became personalized and real for me as a student and later a colleague and friend of Peter F. Drucker.[2] I do not think that Peter ever used the term Systems Thinking in his teaching or writing, but his ability to link the soft sciences with the hard sciences and to communicate that linkage through stories has had a major impact on my thinking, and indeed my life.

Work with Peter Drucker

I took all of Peter's classes and began to know him on a personal level as well. Peter is more than a management guru, teacher, and writer. Peter is a friend, mentor, and role model who, in many respects, changed my life.

Peter Drucker's greatest gift to me, besides that of friendship, was to help me to think from both a historical and a future perspective. Peter has the unique capacity both to understand how the future may be viewed from a historical perspective, as well as to attempt to clarify the future from a range of disciplines; from the social sciences to the physical sciences to what he has designated as the practice of management. Peter does not like the term "holistic" because he doesn't believe that people can agree on what the term means; however, Systems Thinking, cause and effect, feedback and learning are all a part of Peter's frame of reference. Peter opened my eyes and enabled me to view my journey of the study of risk from many different points of view.

WellPoint Health Networks Inc.

In November of 1994, I took early retirement from Deloitte & Touche to join WellPoint Health Networks Inc. as a member of the office of the chairman. My responsibilities included developing a strategic planning process and leading merger integration. I had worked with Leonard Schaeffer, chairman and chief executive officer of WellPoint, since 1985, when he was recruited to turn around what was then Blue Cross of California. Indeed, the WellPoint story will appear as a case study throughout this book.

My two and a half years at WellPoint were extremely useful in my journey of learning. Particularly useful were the decision-making processes that characterize Leonard's management style at both strategic and operational levels. In short, Leonard embraced both a rigorous, fast-based analytic process and a dialogue approach to decision making. Leonard and his executive-level colleagues, including my role, worked very hard at anticipating, understanding, and taking action around issues of the external and enterprise levels, including:

- Public policy.
- Crisis management.
- Regulatory compliance.
- Competition and capital markets.
- Customer relations.
- Human relations.
- Goal-oriented budgeting and actual management.

You will see these phrases repeated as I discuss the Governance Model in succeeding chapters.

I also must give considerable credit to Leonard and his colleagues for helping me learn that the inside perspective on issues is very different from the perception of the same issues from an external point of view. This inside perspective proved to be very useful in the design of the Governance Model and the process for implementation.

Dean, the Peter F. Drucker Graduate School of Management

The president of Claremont Graduate University, Steadman Upham; Peter Drucker; and the faculty of the Drucker School invited me to take a short-term contract to become dean and to help establish a long-term vision and strategic direction for the school. As dean, I had to resign from the doctoral program, but I was privileged to continue my work with Peter and other talented, multidimensional faculty as I kept on with my journey of learning. Being an active member of a graduate university community that focused on literature, music, the arts, and the humanities as well as the social and physical sciences was a personally broadening experience.

During the course of my deanship, I continued my journey of learning and working with Peter until Deloitte & Touche invited me to become a senior advisor in its Enterprise Risk Services (ERS) practice.

Deloitte & Touche Enterprise Risk Services (ERS)

Following my tenure at WellPoint, I continued to work with Deloitte & Touche at the invitation of Bob Rothermel, the managing director of ERS. This relationship with Deloitte & Touche and in particular the ERS group provided me with a platform and forum for my research as well as a group of colleagues and clients with whom I could establish a dialogue to shape and share ideas. I am very grateful to the firm and to Bob not only for providing me with the platform and forum, but also for trusting me, in particular as the journey took us off the beaten path of conventional wisdom. The firm's quest for what we called thought leadership really made this work possible.

With Bob Rothermel's support, we established a task force of professionals who would, in effect, "write the book" on governance and risk. This book was, from the very beginning, my personal goal. In an effort to get it right, to pressure test the ideas, to introduce new concepts, and to share the journey with clients, we enlisted for the task force specialists in various disciplines and industries:

- Capital markets
- Quantitative analysis
- Information technology integrity
- Organizational behavior
- Audit processes
- Corporate governance
- Information security
- Enterprise and business risk management
- Process control improvement

We collected and analyzed data, gathered research materials, and visited companies engaged in many different industries:

- Information systems and software development
- Consumer products
- Financial services
- Health care
- Energy
- Manufacturing
- Retail

During the course of our work together—1999 to 2001—we developed a hypothesis around governance and risk that we informally tested during our interviews and data gathering. Our hypothesis formed the basis for:

- Our definitions of governance, risk, and the Extended Enterprise.
- The application of Systems Thinking.
- The Governance Model.
- The process for implementation.

My formal work ended in the fall of 2001, with an external "thought piece" *Perspectives on Risk* (published as a brochure by Deloitte Touche, 2002). Many of the concepts we developed as a group provided the foundations for the framework and processes outlined in this book as well as a basis for much of the risk consulting practice of Deloitte & Touche.

"Irrational Exuberance"—The Dot-Com Boom and the New Economy

There has probably never been a time since the emergence of the industrial revolution that presented such challenge to the status quo. My journey continued right through the heady days of the maturization of the Internet, the World Wide Web, and the telecom boom. The Internet, the Web, and the fixation on bandwidth created enterprises that did not seem to behave according to anything that any of us had ever before experienced. We believed that a new set of rules would propel us ever upward. As they said in Silicon Valley, "We drank our own Kool-Aid."

During the course of the period that Alan Greenspan, chairman of the Federal Reserve Board, said was characterized by "irrational exuberance," finding an audience upon which to test ideas of governance and risk was very difficult. In an area of unlimited resources, instant paper billionaires, and a cache of Generation X-ers who had never seen a downturn, the topic of governance and risk fell on fairly deaf ears. Even worse, a Governance Model and process that focused on the future consequences of current choices and decisions resulted in glazed looks and polite inattention—except for Peter Drucker.

My Deloitte & Touche colleagues and I visited with Peter a number of times during the development of our thinking. Peter's guidance, criticism, and support were invaluable to the process. For example, as the Governance Model began to take shape, I sent a rough draft of the monograph out to Peter for review and scheduled a visit to receive his feedback and for me to learn. I was very apprehensive about Peter's reaction, particularly around the feasibility of what I believed to be a new way of thinking about the subject. I was greatly relieved when Peter stated:

Only a new point of view has any chance for success. It is the best chance to be heard and listened to. There are too many me-toos.

Peter continued, "The strength of the document is the methodology." However, he went on to comment, "The document is scholarly and conceptual. The thinking has been done. It now requires editing." This work is a result of Peter's edits, as well as input from others acknowledged in this book, feedback from the marketplace, and a continuous dialogue with my colleagues at Deloitte & Touche.

In typical Drucker fashion, Peter took a prophetic look at the future in July 2001:

Management's choices and decisions are coming under more scrutiny than ever before, and management runs a danger of short-term versus long-term thinking.

The issues of governance and risk had come together in Peter's and my thinking when he added:

Risk analysis is a strategic decision and risks must be anticipated.

During the remainder of the dot-com boom, I continued testing the Governance Model on a variety of audiences in an effort to help individuals and organizations to anticipate, understand, and take action around the consequences of their choices and decisions. As the end of 1999 approached, I got more listeners.

Y2K—the Day Nothing Happened!

I have heard many comments about the nonevent of January 1, 2000. Such comments raised issues around wasted spending, false claims, cries of wolf, an excuse for spending the profits of the boom, and a full-employment act for consultants and information technology providers. I believe that the reason nothing happened is a direct result of boards, the government, and all levels of management working solidly for two to three years in an effort to anticipate, understand, and take action around a real threat. Decisions were taken on a global basis to deal with a crisis before it occurred.

I am sure that in an era of large budgets and a mandate to upgrade and replace legacy systems, there was waste. There was an excuse to spend. But look at the alternative. The prophets of doom suggested that everything from nuclear war to global famine would occur. And without a massive global effort, those outcomes were not beyond the realm of possibility. We will never know what would have happened if we had not embarked on the initiatives that we undertook. What did happen was what was supposed to happen—nothing.

The lesson of Y2K reinforced the idea that outcomes of choices and decisions—risks—can be successfully acted upon, even at a global level.

March 2000—the Beginning of the End, or the End of the Beginning?

Nasdaq hit its all-time high of 5,048.62 on March 10, 2000. By the end of 2002, the securities that are traded on Nasdaq had lost 75 percent of their perceived value. What happened, and even more important, would a model of governance and risk have made any difference? The quick answer to the first question is that we had what in any other century would have been termed "a run on the bank." Investors lost confidence. Markets work only if individuals feel that they will be better off tomorrow than they are today. Would a model of governance and risk have made any difference? In most cases, probably not. Governance and risk are logical, rational concepts. Unbridled optimism and a willingness to "drink our own Kool-Aid" are irrational feelings, hence the Fed chairman's observation. We also are inclined to believe what we wish to believe or what is in our perceived best interest to believe, regardless of information, facts, or logic.

The lesson learned once again from the crash of 2000, in addition to the "greater fool" theory and lessons of history, is that boards and executives must continuously think through the consequences of their choices and decisions. They must anticipate, understand, and take action around such consequences just as they did with Y2K. Boards and executive management must understand that history does repeat itself; that there are tools, techniques, and processes available to help reduce the uncertainty of the future; and that outcomes may be much more knowable if we make the effort to look ahead.

2001 ONWARD

This next segment of my journey, including my pause at the present, really served to confirm my earlier learnings. The actual events of the past three years provided a rich set of examples and cases that fit into my emerging framework for thinking about governance and risk.

September 11, 2001—the Ultimate Crisis

For most of us, our lives were forever changed on 9/11. The ultimate crisis occurred. No one could have anticipated specifics of the act of terrorism; however, the contingency planning that took place prior to 9/11 saved thousands of lives. Notwithstanding the loss of 3,000 lives, most of the critical functions of the financial markets and governmental activities were back on line in less than a week.

The lessons of 9/11 and Y2K reinforced my belief that forward thinking in an organized way is effective in minimizing the consequences of events that are beyond our control or comprehension. We need not be the victims of bad luck or chance. We have some degree of choice over our destinies.

The Scandals

No sooner had we begun to stabilize our institutions and confidence following 9/11, when the scandals hit. The popular and business press and television news networks brought home the events of Enron, WorldCom, Tyco, Arthur Andersen, and others in ways that shook the very foundations of our free-market economy. Arrogance, greed, and a sense of entitlement became the symbols of capitalism to many around the world. The excesses and lack of reality of the 1990s were coming home to roost. And, unfortunately, it was the average investor and employee who got hurt versus the boards and executives who used public companies as their personal fiefdoms. The political process overtook the regulatory process in ways not seen since the Great Depression.

Interview with Stephen Cooper   Among the most significant milestones in my journey was a renewal of a long-standing relationship with Steve Cooper, interim CEO of Enron.

Steve also serves as CEO of Zolfo Cooper, a bankruptcy and turn-around firm in New York. Steve has worked with his colleagues on scores of failed companies over the years and was therefore a great source of common themes on the subject of governance and risk. When I met with Steve, I did not explore Enron, partially because there have been several books written on the subject; I was seeking more to understand generic problems common to all failed companies. I therefore asked Steve to help with what he sees as common themes from among all of his experiences. I have interpreted and recorded Steve's observations as follows:

First, Steve characterizes the leadership of most enterprises into two broad categories:

1. Those who have foresight and are proactive.
2. Those who tend to use hindsight and are reactive.

Of course, from Steve's perspective, organizations that are looking forward and constantly adjusting their strategies to achieve a fit with their environment tend to survive and grow. Conversely, those enterprises that are constantly surprised by changes in the environment tend to believe that everything and everyone is the problem except themselves. Indeed, Steve's sense is that the overarching problem found in most enterprises that ultimately fail is that of entitlement and greed. In fact, the longer the tenure of many CEOs, the greater their sense of entitlement—"I created all of this, and as a result I am entitled to take whatever I wish." Greed is the outcome of this misplaced sense of entitlement.

Taking that characteristic of entitlement and greed a step further, Steve observed that the CEO and senior management often lose touch with reality and along with that failure and believing themselves no longer accountable for their own actions are quick to blame conditions they believe are beyond their control for the misfortunes of themselves and their organizations.

When I inquired further into the details of the characteristics of most failed enterprises, Steve organized his comments into two main categories:

1. Missing the megawaves—just not seeing them coming, including:
   - Governmental interventions.
   - Technological innovations.
   - Competition.

2. Operational, executional, and financial failures, including:
   - ■ Wandering from core competencies.
   - ■ Unplanned growth, including roll-ups, misunderstood synergies, and a failure to block and tackle.
   - ■ Management denial, including a lack of foresight and insight, prevalence of hindsight and reactive behavior, and an unwillingness to deal with legacy costs, indeed deferring such problems and costs of successors.
   - ■ Accountability and blame, including a lack of acceptance of personal accountability and a willingness to place blame on others.
   - ■ Indispensable CEO.
   - ■ Situations in which corporate governance is lost, and "boards become prisoners of war."
   - ■ Disconnect between pay and performance.
   - ■ Pressures on expectations, short-term performance.

Steve had an interesting sports analogy around outcomes and metrics. In Steve's view sports results are recorded in real time—as they occur. Business results, like the outcomes of sporting events, should also be recorded in real time—as they occur.

Regarding current events around corporate governance, it is Steve's opinion that the CEO should not be on the board and that the board should have its own staff—in particular, financial analysts.

Finally, as I did with most of my interviews, I asked Steve to give me his definitions of risk:

- ■ Worst-case scenario from a particular transaction.
- ■ Probability of outcomes.
- ■ Consequences of choices and decisions.
- ■ Stupid, short-term decisions in the name of growth.

Indeed, as I reflected on Steve's comments and integrated them into my own framework of governance and risk, I drew the following conclusions.

First, the issue of leadership of successful enterprises tended to center around the ability and willingness of boards and senior management to anticipate, understand, and take action around their choices and related decisions, and the consequences of such choices and decisions.

Conversely, those organizations that got into difficulty were characterized by an unwillingness or inability of boards and senior management to look outward and to contemplate the megatrends and at the same time to look inward to objectively examine the lessons of history in terms of current attitudes and behavior.

Second, the characteristics of most failed enterprises, sooner or later, seem to center around arrogance and greed as a characteristic tone at the top. Companies fail from the top down, not the other way around. Each of the failures that I experienced during my journey had more to do with a leadership style characterized by a failure to listen and learn than outright incompetence.

Steve's observations were very helpful and much appreciated. You will see many of his thoughts carried forward throughout this book.

The scandals and the political drive for reform in the name of corporate governance established new layers of regulatory compliance without necessarily addressing the underlying core issues that caused the scandals in the first place. New laws and the resulting regulations defined governance in ways that do not address the basic problems, but probably serve to make the problems worse. This idea of the cure being worse than the disease unfortunately has side effects or unintended consequences:

- Processes are put in place that divert attention from the real issues of governance.
- Excessive regulation places a huge burden on small to midsize public companies that generally fuel economic growth.

The important learning for boards and executives from the scandals and the resulting compliance requirements is that of maintaining focus on the real issues of governance and risk and not becoming lured into a false sense of security that something is being done that will make a difference. In the words of Bill Longbrake, "What you do about these issues is good management and a failure to deal with these matters is bad management."

Three Cases

During the course of my journey, I was privileged to work with three very different organizations that helped to refine my concepts of governance and risk to the Governance Model. The companies are:

- Washington Mutual (WaMu).
- Physicians Mutual Insurance Company (PMIC).
- WellPoint Health Networks Inc. (WLP).

Washington Mutual Under the strategic guidance and leadership of Kerry Killinger, CEO, WaMu emerged from a mutual savings and loan (S&L) to the largest thrift institution in the United States. WaMu, now a public company with a market capitalization of over $30 billion, has become a national powerhouse in consumer financial services, including retail banking and residential mortgages. During the course of my journey, I made several trips to corporate headquarters to meet with senior executives, including Kerry Killinger and Bill Longbrake. Kerry provided the vision for the institution, including the strategy for growth through acquisition, while Bill, as vice chairman, put in place the frameworks for governance and risk. A Ph.D. in finance, Bill intuitively embraced the concept of risk being an outcome of choices and decisions and immediately set about putting in place the processes for implementation over 20 years ago.

Not only did WaMu embrace the concepts of governance and risk, but the firm also implemented those concepts from its early days under Kerry's leadership. For example, the commitment of WaMu to long-term share owner value avoided many of the pitfalls of short-term thinking and decision making that produced the consequences that became the S&L crisis of the 1980s.

WaMu was an early adapter of a powerful set of core values that created the Tone at the Top introduced earlier. Those values are, if anything, more relevant today than they were when they were put in place 20 years ago:

- Ethics—All actions are guided by absolute honesty, integrity, and fairness.
- Respect—People are valued and appreciated for their contributions.
- Teamwork—Cooperation, trust, and shared objectives are vital to success.
- Innovation—New ideas are encouraged and sound strategies implemented with enthusiasm.
- Excellence—High standards for service and performance are expected and rewarded.

Finally, WaMu has adopted the principles of governance and risk to its organization and decision-making processes by continuously changing and seeking a good fit with the external environment.

WaMu is a great example of an enterprise that processes feedback and learning to achieve continuous improvement. When one considers that the overarching strategy for growth has been through acquisitions, such learning is imperative.

I am very grateful to Kerry and Bill for sharing their ideas and experiences with me and for providing feedback on my emerging thinking.

Physicians Mutual   As long-time consulting clients, the senior executives of this Omaha-based mutual life and health insurance company were quick to embrace the Governance Model as a vehicle for implementing transitional change within the organization.

PMIC was 100 years old in 2002 as the Governance Model implementation process entered its second year. This highly rated institution provides supplementary life, health, and annuity products. During the course of its 100-year history, PMIC developed considerable competencies in direct marketing and the management of the risks associated with marketing to its customers. The strategic risks faced by the company included a focus on one or two products and channels of distribution in an environment of increased competition. The primary risks, therefore, were associated with its future viability as a company with a narrow focus on products and distribution.

The strategy formulation process was the first phase of the implementation of the Governance Model and actually began in 1997. The execution of the strategy through a rigorous business planning process was initiated in 2001. The operational planning and budgeting process had been implemented some years earlier.

The PMIC President's Council, which consists of the president and CEO, executive vice president and COO, executive vice president and CFO, and senior vice president, Direct Marketing Group, established a strategy to enable the company to become customer-focused and to operate through business units. These business units, led by two senior vice presidents, established the execution phase of the transition to the governance model.

The Governance Model and related process of implementation worked quite well as evidenced by feedback from the executive committee—the top 20 officers of the company. While improvements are necessary and will be carried out in the next planning cycle, the system is thought to be working well and is serving the purpose of anticipating, understanding, and taking action around the consequences of choices available and decisions taken.

An important take-away point from this case is the fact that the Governance Model served as the framework and process for change management. This point will be emphasized in greater detail in Chapter 10, "Making It Happen."

I am very grateful to Robert Reed, president and CEO, and his colleagues for working very hard and being extremely supportive in the implementation of the Governance Model. The feedback and learning during this portion of my journey contributed considerably to the concepts incorporated in this book.

WellPoint Health Networks Inc.   During the course of my journey, I paid a return visit to WellPoint. You will see WellPoint appear several times throughout this book as the source of illustrations that support Big Decisions. The WellPoint story from a historical perspective will be told elsewhere; however, for the purpose of testing my ideas around governance and risk, interviews with Leonard D. Schaeffer, chairman and CEO, and Thomas C. Geiser, executive vice president and general counsel, are cited here. The template for my interviews centered around decisions and choices including:

- Organizational awareness, anticipation, and understanding.
- Decision-making process, leadership styles, and models.
- Execution, strategy, and action.
- Outcomes and results.
- Learning; acquiring and transferring knowledge.

The learnings are integrated into the chapters that follow; however, a quote from each person helps to affirm the direction of my journey and the nature of decision making:

Leonard: "At least half of our success has resulted from what we chose not to do, particularly acquisitions and Medicare-related business."

Tom: "What you are presenting is a framework to facilitate the freedom of thought (choices) not constrained by risks (outcomes)."

My thanks to Leonard and Tom and the entire WellPoint team, who have set the standard for sound decision making.

The Uncertainty

How should boards and executives think about the future in a world that may be characterized as being more uncertain than ever before? From the perspective of governance and risk, the operative words must be:

- Anticipation
- Understanding
- Action

around the consequences of choices and decisions. As individuals and organizations, we cannot predict the future. What we can do is look ahead from as many points of view as possible. Boards and executives must take as much, if not more, responsibility for foresight as they are being required to do with hindsight.

The subject of uncertainty, or at least the degrees of uncertainty, helped to guide the development of the Governance Model that is the foundation for this book. Through a series of sessions with Peter Drucker, we established the idea of degrees of uncertainty. We decided to use the idea of what is unknown, knowable, and known for establishing a framework for considering uncertainty. Coupled with the basic concepts of Systems Thinking, the perspective of degrees of uncertainty enabled the Governance Model to begin to take shape.

LESSONS LEARNED

As related earlier, the past 17 years have been a journey of discovery. The journey is not over. No final destination has been reached. The learning will never end. The years from 1985 to 2003, however, have provided the richest time in our history for learning, testing, and framing which may help boards of directors and executives fulfill their roles. Having survived the white water of change thus far, what learnings has the journey produced?

- There is no consistent definition or understanding of the words "governance" and "risk." Very few of the people with whom I spoke and very little of the research I conducted dealt with the meaning of either word.
- There is a universal attempt to manage effects, outcomes, or results versus a willingness to deal with inputs and causes. One cannot touch or manage a result; one can only manage *for* a result. The only situations in which outcomes, for example financial results, can be directly managed are when manipulation of those final outcomes has occurred—that is, cheating.
- There is no organized body of knowledge that may be taught, implemented, reviewed, or attested to on the subjects of governance and risk.
- There is very little organizational learning of a structured nature that takes place as a result of feedback or rigorous assessment of the outcomes or results of decisions taken throughout an enterprise.
- Financial institutions are different. Financial services institutions tend to integrate the risks of being an intermediary—for example, trading, credit, underwriting, or hedging—with business risks. This integration complicates decisions around the business itself with the infinite detail and complexity of the intermediary role.

Everything I have reviewed and learned in the course of my journey either provides examples of what is required to be compliant or deals with risk as a static assessment.

No Consistent Definition of "Governance" and "Risk"

Here are various definitions of governance and risk drawn from Internet sources including Wikipedia, WordNet 1.7 Vocabulary Helper, and Ask Jeeves:

What Is Governance?

- The exercise of **control**.
- The act, process, or **power** of governing.
- State of being **governed**.
- The act, process, manner, or **power** of exercising **authority** and **control**.
- Exercise of **authority**; **control**; arrangement.
- The persons, committees, or departments who make up a governing body and who **administer** something.
- The act of exercising **authority**.

What Is Risk?

- Possibility of suffering harm or loss.
- A factor, thing, element, or course involving uncertain danger.
- The danger of probability of loss to an insurer.
- The variability of returns from an investment.
- Someone or something that creates or suggests a hazard.
- Gamble, liability, speculation, uncertainty, venture.
- A venture undertaken without regard to possible loss or injury.
- **The potential future harm that may arise from some present action.**
- The unanticipatable likelihood of loss or less than expected return.
- Uncertainty or variability.
- Standard deviation of the return on total investment; degree of uncertainty of return on an asset.

The single reference to risk as an outcome is in boldface.

I also inquired into Encycogov.com, "The Encyclopedia about Corporate Governance," and was presented with multiple definitions because of so many special interests in the field. One definition put forth by Encycogov.com was helpful in terms of associating governance and decision making:

> *Corporate governance is the system by which business corporations are directed and controlled. The corporate governance structure specifies the distribution of rights and responsibilities among different participants in the corporation, such as the board, managers, shareholders, and other stakeholders, and spells out the rules and procedures for making decisions on corporate affairs. By doing this, it also provides the structure through which the company objectives are set, and the means of attaining those objectives and monitoring performance. (Organization for Economic Cooperation and Development, April 1999)*

My interviews and seminars provided little further enlightenment on governance. Such ideas as responsibility or serving the interests of shareholders were mentioned but little discussion took place around responsibility for what, or how such responsibility might be carried out.

When discussing the subject of risk, certain words have typically come to mind:

- Threat
- Opportunity
- Nothing ventured, nothing gained
- Insurance
- Crises

The only time the words "probable outcomes" were used was in the context of a mathematical definition of risk.

The questions I kept asking throughout my journey of discovery were:

- *What is governance?*
- *What is risk?*

The conclusion of this chapter will introduce definitions that when taken together form the basis for a framework that deals with both questions.

We all recognize that we live in a cause-and-effect world. There are results from each and every action we take. Yet when we refer to either term, governance or risk, we are provided only with a view of the result. We are not schooled in the laws of unintended consequences. We are not engaged to understand the cause or input that produced such results.

Examples of strategic risks are offered in terms of declining profit margins or product obsolescence. Those are clearly outcomes or risks, but they are the result of an input or a cause that is not established. Governance is communicated in terms of the characteristics of "good" or "bad" governance practices of "good" or "bad" boards. Examples that depict independence of board members, hiring of external auditors, financial competence, and owning (or not owning) shares or options are all illustrations of what a regulatory body determines to be good governance. The issue of how good governance is actually exercised is generally not addressed. Again, we witness a focus on a result, not a cause or the input that produced that result.

Why are we giving all this attention to cause and effect? If we cannot or do not focus on why things happen the way they do or why things go wrong, we run the great risk of solving the wrong problem. The relationship between cause and effect is extremely complex, and a failure to recognize the law of unintended consequences, I believe, is at the root of most of our issues around governance and risk.

No Body of Knowledge on Governance and Risk

Boards and executives have no source for gaining information and knowledge around the implementation of programs that deal with the real issues of governance and risk. Graduate schools of business and associations conduct seminars and workshops on corporate governance, and there are programs to certify that boards practice good governance. These programs, and I have attended and conducted many, are useful and create important awareness around the subject. They represent what I call the necessary but not sufficient information that boards and executives require. What is missing, I believe, is a framework and process for simultaneously dealing with both subjects—governance and risk—in one model. Also missing is a process for implementation—a shortcoming I hope to remedy in Chapter 10. Hopefully, this milestone in my journey will provide at least the beginning of a framework that may then be used and improved upon.

Very Little Organizational Learning

Finally, improvement in any activity requires feedback and learning to take place. In the dynamic cause-and-effect world in which we live, feedback and learning must occur if we are to improve and grow as individuals and as organizations. Of course, the most successful organizations, let's say the top 20 percent of any population, are constantly improving and growing. For the majority of enterprises, however, any improvement and any growth are temporary. These are many reasons for this phenomenon that I call "organizational porpoising." A constant focus on short-term results is often cited as the principal culprit; however, I believe that explanation is merely another focus on outcome. Organizations that do not systematically process feedback and assess the outcomes of their decisions not only are subject to repeating their mistakes, they have no clue as to what works and what does not work. Organizations that do not track the intended and unintended consequences of their decisions are constantly subject to the idea of the week and the latest management fads as opposed to gaining a deep understanding of how their decisions may produce desired outcomes.

Financial Services Organizations as Intermediaries

As I pointed out in my 1985–1992 discussion of a risk assessment framework and process that did not work, the risk-bearing nature of a financial services institution presents a set of unique challenges to governance and risk. While all enterprises are risk-bearing in one way or another, banks, insurance companies, brokerage firms, and other special-purpose financial institutions present two major complexities to issues of governance and risk:

1. The business itself—that is, how the enterprise interacts with its environment to survive and grow.
2. The unique organization, processes, and informational risks associated with being a financial institution.

In my experience, integrating these two characteristics of governance and risk, particularly in a large, complex financial institution, results in a set of structures that are virtually unmanageable. Generally speaking, since the primary business of a financial service organization is that of a risk-bearing intermediary, such activities become the focus of the majority of the governance and risk initiatives. Such a focus is, of course, important; however, a focus on the business as a business is also critical. For this reason, it is my belief that the two issues should have two separate but equal models of governance and risk.

CONCLUSION

What are the implications of the Lessons Learned? First, definitions of the terms "governance" and "risk." Once I realized that in a cause-and-effect world risk is an outcome of choices available and decisions taken, it became clear to me that true governance is really the process of decision making under various degrees of certainty or uncertainty. In other words, governance and decision making are the cause, risk, and reward—the effect or the outcome of those decisions. The convergence of governance and risk became the basis for all that followed. The 17-year journey reached a milestone upon which a framework and process could be developed. The following definitions brought it all together for me:

> *What Is Governance?*
> Corporate governance is not, as its core, about power, it is about finding ways to ensure that decisions are made effectively.—John Pound[3]

> *What Is Risk?*
> Risk (and reward) is the outcome of choices available and decisions taken.

General Systems Theory and Systems Thinking enabled the gradual development of the Governance Model and the process for implementation to take place. It was clearly not sufficient to stop and declare that governance was all about decision making and that risks and rewards were the outcomes or results of those decisions. A framework and process that could provide boards and executive management with the toolbox for organizing the decision-making processes and facilitating feedback and learning had to be developed. The Governance Model and the process for implementation will hopefully provide boards and executives with that toolbox.

NOTES

1. Peter F. Drucker, *The Practice of Management* (New York: Harper-Collins, 1986).
2. Peter F. Drucker, professor of management, Peter F. Drucker Graduate School of Management, Claremont Graduate University, Claremont, CA. Peter is quoted throughout this work through numerous conversations with the author.
3. John Pound, *The Promise of the Governed Corporation*, *Harvard Business Review* (March–April 1995).

CHAPTER 2

A Current Perspective: Why Things Go Wrong

INTRODUCTION

In Chapter 1, I described the 17-year journey of discovery that for me brought the subjects of governance and risk together. Those subjects, as I related, did not start out together but came together as the journey progressed. I could no longer think about them separately. When I considered risk and reward, I thought about outcomes or results of choices and decisions. When I considered governance, I thought about the processes for making decisions from among choices. When I thought about governance and risk together, I thought about a framework for evaluating the intended and unintended consequences of choices and decisions and a process for implementation.

As I considered ways to approach the logic and writing of this book to make it a useful guide to members of boards and executive management, I felt the need to define the problem we are trying to solve. The fact that my colleagues and I took a trip together and arrived at Milestone 17—a model for governance and risk—did not mean that the reader, traveling a different path, would arrive at the same milestone. At this point in the journey, in order for others to come to their own conclusions about governance and risk, it seems to me that we need a common starting point—the "problem." That is, how do we perceive the problems of governance and risk that we are attempting to solve? This chapter is also intended to explain why things don't work out the way we think they will, as well as why we are continuously surprised when things go wrong. Today's problems with governance and risk and why things go wrong are described from two points of view:

- Conventional wisdom—The so-called "general agreement among parties" regarding *what* we think about governance and risk.
- Fragmentation—*How* we are organized to perform the required governance and management activities.

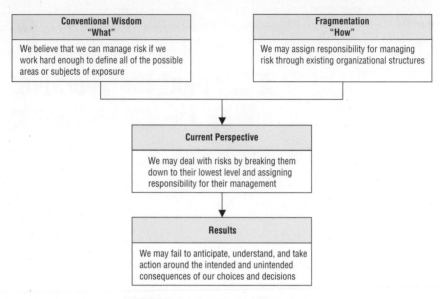

FIGURE 2.1   Our Current Perspective

As a starting point for my efforts at problem definition and as a guide to the logic of this chapter, I created Figure 2.1 as a flow diagram that positions conventional wisdom and fragmentation as the two drivers of our current paradigm or perspective on governance and risk. In summary, the current perspective yields the result we have experienced:

> *Failure to anticipate, understand, and take action around the intended and unintended consequences of our choices and decisions.*

Let me digress for a moment and give you my view of the starting point of our current perspective and its result.

SIR ISAAC NEWTON'S PERSPECTIVE AND ITS IMPLICATIONS

The roots of both conventional wisdom and fragmentation spring from the same seed—Sir Isaac Newton. We will discuss how Sir Isaac's theories of 300 years ago took root and formed our perception of both the *what* and the *how* of governance and risk.

Sir Isaac Newton was probably the most profound thinker of his day, if not any day, until Albert Einstein. Without attempting to do justice to

Newton's legacy, it is important to our understanding of the current perspective to recognize the origins of that perspective. Newton's worldview not only lasted 300 years, it profoundly affects how we look at the world today. Newton held that the universe consisted of countless uniform particles or fragments held together by gravity. Further, Newton and others who followed held the view that the universe was one big "machine," governed by immutable laws that would be used to explain all perspectives of science, philosophy, psychology, and social phenomena. Newton also asserted that all of the homogeneous particles that formed his mechanical view of the universe not only fit together, they moved together without regard for space or time, and were created by God.

The bottom line of this snapshot into Newtonian history is this: We learned, as did our predecessors over the past 300 years, that we could understand an issue or a problem by breaking it down or reducing it to its component pieces, fixing the pieces, and putting the "machine" back together again. Hence the term "mechanistic" or "reductionist" thinking. Thanks to Sir Isaac Newton, we have a perspective, a point of view, on the way things work and how we solve problems. Sir Isaac's perspective led to the industrial revolution; to the worker efficiency observations of Frederick W. Taylor; to Henry Ford's assembly line; and to much of the economic and political "miracles" of the past 100 years in developed nations, such as the continuous improvement programs found in much of Japanese industry.

Modern science has proved Sir Isaac's perspective to be if not incorrect, to be at least incomplete. During the twentieth century, Newtonian physics—and perspective—gave way to quantum mechanics (atoms and molecules), the Theory of Relativity (time and space), and the notion of the observer and the observed (we are a part of what we see). Modern science brought us the nuclear age as well as a different perspective around how and why things work the way they do. Interestingly though, for most of us, our perspective on the way things work is still strongly grounded in Newtonian physics—the way we used to think things worked. In other words, reality around the way things actually work and our perspective around how we think they work are very different. It is no wonder, then, that our conventional wisdom is something from the past. So, too, is our perspective.

DOES OUR PERSPECTIVE MATTER?

Does all of this discussion around perspective and "why things go wrong" matter? Do we have to throw out how we think about how things work and adopt a new, unfamiliar, perhaps even unproven point of view? The quick answer is *no*! A lot of what used to work still works. The assembly line and interchangeability of parts still work; organizations that divide and assign accountability and responsibility for tasks still work; breaking down a problem into its component parts still helps to solve the problem. It is just that in the ever increasing complexity of the world we live in, the old way of looking at "why things go wrong" or, for that matter, "why they go right" is not complete.

WHAT COMES NEXT?

What then do we have to do? I believe that we have to handle two points of view or perspectives at the same time. That is the hard part! Juggling the perspective we grew up with while adding a perhaps new and different point of view, and being able to draw comparisons between the two, will really help to gain a better understanding of both "why things go wrong" and "why things really work the way they do."

What I am asking you to do is not put the book down while uttering with exasperation, "Here is another how-to book on change management." I am not trying to change you or your organization—I can't do that. Nobody but you can do that. What I am trying to do is open up the aperture on your lens to take in more light, and enable you to view what you see in a broader frame. I am asking you to open up and consider another (not a substitute) way of looking at a problem. If you don't like what you see, you can always go back to your original perspective.

CONVENTIONAL WISDOM—A GENERAL AGREEMENT AMONG PARTIES

I believe that one of the great challenges to creativity, innovation, and the implementation of new ideas is what some call conventional wisdom or "groupthink." This challenge was painfully present as I attempted to apply the concepts of Systems Thinking to the subjects of governance and risk.

What Do We Mean by the Words "Conventional Wisdom"?

Conventional wisdom is basically those ideas or concepts that "everyone" knows to be true. Others may call conventional wisdom "groupthink." Any idea that everybody knows or acknowledges to be the case is always suspect. An example is the often quoted dictum, "If you can't measure it, you can't manage it." Think about how often you have heard, or perhaps repeated, that phrase when trying to put in place metrics around an activity. The fact is, although there are some activities, particularly in the management of physical processes, that may be both measured and managed, many other attributes of human behavior may be managed only indirectly or cannot be measured at all, as in the case of values or motivation. However, conventional wisdom on the subject of measurement and management flatly states, "If you can't measure it, you can't manage it." Conventional wisdom is misleading.

Conventional wisdom generally becomes misleading simply because by the time everybody is in agreement, the subject and the situation have changed. Said another way, conventional wisdom is yesterday's wisdom. What is needed is a different way of thinking about governance and risk—a way that does not reflect the consensus of the past but rather provides a framework for considering the future.

John Carl, the former Senior Vice President and Chief Financial Officer of Allstate Insurance Company, added an interesting and helpful perspective on the subject of conventional wisdom. John introduced the biological concept of imprinting as a way of describing a corporate culture that fosters consistency of thinking across the enterprise. As John described the phenomenon of imprinting, he used the example of the first person that one worked for as placing an imprint on one's future beliefs, behavior, and attitudes. When you think about it, large organizations are cast with the imprint of their early leaders. Imprinting produces conventional wisdom and groupthink.

Just What Is the Conventional Wisdom about Governance?

A few of the current perspectives on the subject of governance were introduced in Chapter 1. When I conduct workshops on governance and risk, I often ask the participants to share their views, which I record on flip charts at the beginning of the session. When conducting research for this book I am constantly looking for current perspectives. Interpreting individual views on what constitutes good corporate governance is a little like the story of the elephant and the blindfolded people. Each individual describes what he or she feels and further assumes that those assumptions are held by everyone else.

Conventional wisdom about governance, like the elephant, depends on the perspective of the beholder. There are generally two lines of thinking put forth when the subject is broached:

1. Compliance
2. Responsibility

Compliance with regulations and perhaps even best practices is what I have referred to as the necessary but not sufficient criterion for good governance. In fact, and unfortunately, good governance is often limited to compliance. The two are not the same.

Responsibility, on the other hand, is often mentioned in terms of shareholders. Boards of directors, of course, have a fiduciary responsibility to serve the interests of shareholders. Most often, that responsibility is deemed to be exercised through compliance with regulations and so-called best practices. But responsibilities of boards go far beyond compliance. Indeed, the responsibilities of boards go not only beyond compliance, they extend to all stakeholders, including owners, employees, customers, suppliers, communities, and network partners.

Like any broad, general statement, there are exceptions. During the course of my research, there were different perspectives put forth that were not what I would call conventional wisdom. For example, the quotation of John Pound, formerly of the Harvard Law School, cited in Chapter 1 defined the governance role of the board in a very unconventional way. The sub-Council on Corporate Governance and the Markets—part of the Council on Competitiveness set up by President George H.W. Bush in 1992, and which is cited in greater depth in the Chapter 1—also dealt with the roles of the board in ways that one could not classify as conventional wisdom. Indeed, during my journey, such references were extremely helpful in establishing my own perspectives on governance and the role of boards of directors.

Just What Is the Conventional Wisdom about Risk?

The concept of risk management has come a long way since the advent of the London insurance markets of 300 years ago. The evolution of the concept of risk management moved from insurance to financial risks such as interest, duration, and market and became the domain of the chief financial officer, who laid off some of those risks into the capital and insurance markets. Other risks were "retained and managed."

As time passed and our thinking on risk developed, we recognized that the traditional views of risk—that is, what most people thought—were no longer sufficient. Conventional wisdom which, for the most part, considered individual occurrences of risk, needed to be taken to a new level.

THE REALITY—ONE CANNOT DIRECTLY MANAGE OUTCOMES

Abandoning conventional wisdom leads to the ultimate consequence that real risks are not only nearly impossible to define, they are equally impossible to directly manage. For example, an organization may be expected to manage outcomes such as:

- Product or service quality.
- Customer and employee satisfaction.
- A new market or product initiative.
- A major systems initiative.
- Reputation and brand equity.
- Values and culture.
- Suppliers and alliance partners.

How does an organization manage outcomes such as these, as well as the impact that any one of these elements has on other outcomes? All of these topics are outcomes or results of choices and decisions made under various conditions of uncertainty. None of these elements may be directly managed as risks, yet conventional wisdom and most of the current literature on risk says that we can and must manage such outcomes. The problem we are trying to solve is not so much a problem of governance and risk, but a problem of perception, and how we attempt to deal with that problem.

At the root of our discussion and as I related in Chapter 1, the reality that attempting to manage risk by establishing categories of risk does not achieve the intended purpose. The categories of risk outlined in the literature on the subject all look pretty much alike. Some lists are longer than others and have different structures, but the common theme among them is that they all deal with results, effects, or outcomes, not the sources, causes, or inputs that produced them. Conventional wisdom looks at risk as a finite "menu" of "stuff" that could happen rather than a model of choices and decisions that have results or outcomes that may or may not be knowable. Outcomes and results and, therefore, risks and rewards cannot be directly managed.

Cause and Effect

Let's examine this idea of cause and effect a little more closely. If we were to make a list of effects or results, which are really the types of risks we face, we would most likely see the following major categories:

- Operational risk
- Business risk
- Market risk
- Financial risk
- Credit/counterparty risk

- Privacy risk
- Political risk
- Legal/regulatory risk
- Environmental risk

The details within each category are nearly infinite—the lists go on and on. All of the categories are the results of everything we do, or don't do; decisions we make, or don't make. Let's take, for example, market risk as a major category and drill down into a few other risks that comprise that category:

- Market share
- Pricing
- Product obsolescence

How does one manage the result or risk called market share? Market share is the result of not only our actions but those of our existing and emerging competitors, regulators, and suppliers, not to mention those actions of our customers. Such actions are often widely separated in space and time from the final outcome. We cannot directly manage market share risk because we cannot manage all of the choices and decisions—outcomes—as well as the consequences of those choices, not to mention their final impact on the market. *All we can manage are the decisions we make from the choices available to us. We may anticipate, understand, and take action around the consequences of our decisions and imagine the choices and decisions that may be made by others, and little more.*

Is the Issue Self-Evident?

The questions I keep asking myself as I think about the dilemma of *what* problem we are trying to solve are: Is the cause and effect idea so obvious that it is already embedded in everyone's thinking? Is this idea what the academics call a tautology, a circular concept that is self-evident and merely proves itself? Is it totally obvious that bad decisions lead to bad outcomes and bad outcomes are the result of bad decisions? First, if one could directly map decisions with results, the idea of cause and effect might be self-evident. The fact is we cannot directly map decisions with results. Not only are there too many factors that influence results, but results generally show up in a different space and time than the inputs that produced them. Risks rarely occur as a direct result of the choices and decisions that produced them.

Said another way, trying to manage outcomes or results, or trying to manage what could be wrong, is like looking through a telescope from the wrong end. You take away a distorted image. Looking at why things may go wrong and trying to reverse engineer back to the causes of what might happen is impossible. However, a careful examination of how the various levels of uncertainty of our choices and decisions may play out over time gets us much closer to the root of what might go wrong.

Then What?

What can we manage, if not outcomes or results? We can manage the choices and decisions available to us. We can anticipate, understand, and take action around the consequences of such choices and decisions. The Governance Model we introduce in Chapter 5 does just that. We establish our categories for decision making based on the uncertainty of outcomes.

- Strategy—outcomes associated with the future.
- Execution—outcomes that are, or should be, knowable.
- Operations—outcomes associated with the present.

FRAGMENTATION—HOW WE DEAL WITH GOVERNANCE AND RISK

As we see in Figure 2.1, fragmentation is the second major problem or driver of our current perspective. Fragmentation, as a basis for our current perspective, leads us to believe that we may deal with risk by assigning organizational responsibility for managing each category of risk that could be identified.

As discussed earlier in this chapter, the Isaac Newton perspective of 300 years ago taught us how to solve a problem or fix an object by reducing or breaking the problem into its component parts, fixing the parts, and then putting the parts of the "machine" back together again. That same perspective has led us to the organizational structures we have designed to deal with the complexities of our modern enterprises as they confront against their environments.

The classic or generic organization chart, Figure 2.2, describes how work and risk are typically divided. The work of the enterprise is carried out by individuals assigned the accountability and responsibility for tasks and, as is often the case, held responsible also for managing the risks inherent within those tasks. Most activities are managed within the

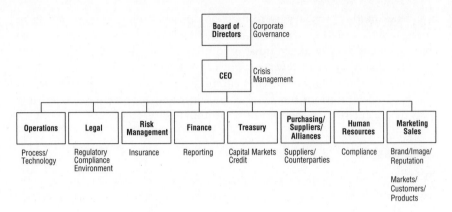

FIGURE 2.2   The Classic Organization

organizational "silos," and so, too, are most risks. As a result, we look at the pieces and do not see the whole. And, as you might expect, the pieces, even when viewed horizontally across the silos, do not complete the whole.

What Is Wrong with This Picture?

In a lot of ways, the silos—or what I call the fragmented approach to work and risk—was very helpful. The so-called classic organizational structure stood for nearly 100 years. Linking the management of risk to the existing framework also worked pretty well until the external world and the concept of the Extended Enterprise began to create surprises and failures that we had never before experienced.

What happened? The reality that all parts of the Extended Enterprise are interconnected, both inside and outside, resulted in events that surfaced and were dealt with in one part of the organization having an impact somewhere else inside or outside of the enterprise. The greater the degree of interconnectedness, the less the historic ways of looking at organization and risk worked. Things happened that not only surprised us, but were seemingly beyond our control. Today's failures are not nearly as contained within the enterprise as we assumed that they were a generation ago. Today's failures have enormous fallout not only across the Extended Enterprise, but across the global economy. For example, look what happened as a result of the near failure of Long Term Capital Management, the Greenwich, Connecticut, hedge fund. The failure of the Russian bond market nearly brought down the firm as well as provided a significant threat to world financial markets.

CONCLUSION

I have tried in this chapter to define the problem, that is, our current perceptions around governance and risk. The problem is one of perspective—*what* risk is and *how* we deal with issues of governance and risk.

Our perceptions make it very difficult, and in some cases impossible, to see things differently or to hold alternative views. Perception is reality, as they say. Of course, there is always more than one reality.

My challenge in writing this book is the reality that perspectives and perception are deeply held by all of us. My dilemma, given how deeply such views are held, is to convince you to hold, even temporarily, an alternative view. In that alternative view there is hope for a solution to my dilemma. Indeed, this book is all about the possibility that a framework and process for considering governance and risk will produce results that will make a difference.

CHAPTER 3

Changing the Perspective: Why Things Really Happen the Way They Do

INTRODUCTION

This chapter deals with the future—how we might consider the issues of governance and risk with a different perspective. This chapter picks up from the problem we stated in the previous chapter:

> *Failure to anticipate, understand, and take action around the intended and unintended consequences of our choices and decisions.*

and begins to move toward a solution. In this case, our solution is really the consideration of an additional perspective on governance and risk and a framework for implementation. We have challenged the conventional wisdom around *what* constitutes governance and risk as well as the traditional, fragmented organizational structure around *how* risk is managed in most enterprises. Now, we want to replace conventional wisdom and traditional structures with something else—something that goes a long way toward explaining why things really happen the way they do.

I will be introducing the topic of Systems Thinking[1] as a way of portraying the logic between choices and decisions and their relationship to risks and rewards. Systems Thinking is the additional perspective we believe enables an enterprise to anticipate, understand, and take action around the consequences of the choices available and the decisions that need to be made. Systems Thinking provides the framework for the Governance Model, which is at the core of our recommendation for dealing with both *what* constitutes risk and the *how* of implementation.

Systems Thinking casts conventional wisdom in a different light—the idea of cause and effect with continuous feedback and learning. Systems

Thinking provides a framework for dealing with choices and decisions as well as the intended and unintended consequences of those choices and decisions.

WHAT IS SYSTEMS THINKING?
FROM NEWTON TO EINSTEIN

Before we jump in and begin our discussion, I would like to explain why looking at the world from a high level and from a conceptual, theoretical perspective is important. It seems to me that if we can't get our minds around the big picture first, all we really see is the pieces. As you will recall from the preceding chapter, part of our problem is that of fragmentation. We never see the whole. Yet it is only through seeing the whole that we are able to perceive how the pieces fit together and figure out what is missing. I had a client years ago that insisted that if we worried about today's retail sales "flash report" the future would take care of itself. That multibillion-dollar retailer is history.

Most of us, certainly those of us who have our roots in Western culture and language, think and write from left to right. Our brains, particularly our "left brains," are programmed to see the world in terms of linear relationships. We are taught to read words from left to right to make sentences. Our sentence structure moves from noun to verb to noun—"Spot saw John." Our way of looking at problems moves from left to right—A leads to B. Seldom do we consider the circular relationship between B and A.

Systems Thinking introduces the idea of connections and feedback and organizational learning. At the highest level, Systems Thinking teaches us not to view problems or issues in isolation or to reduce or fragment how we look at the world, but to recognize that everything is connected to everything else. Not only are we connected, but the feedback and learning that occurs among and between us changes us. We are taught to view the world in a linear, left-to-right way; however, the reality of the world is circular and interconnected between cause and effect and feedback and learning.

Whose Reality?

Sir Isaac Newton brought us a long way toward an understanding of how things work. Albert Einstein, Richard Feynman, David Boem, and others of the early to mid-twentieth century created a different world-view—the view of quantum mechanics, relativity, and the interconnectedness of it all. Current thinking may not be the end of science as some have hypothesized, but at least that current thinking sheds more light on the way things really work and why things don't work out the way we think they should.

General Systems Theory, which is derived from mid-twentieth-century physics, particularly at MIT, and specifically by Jay Forrester, led to the current worldview of Systems Thinking. That worldview, now further refined by Peter Senge and others, has shaped much of the framework for thinking about risk presented in this book.[2]

A final note on Systems Thinking: I searched for answers to the basic question, "Why don't things work out the way I thought they would or should?" for the first half of my career. As a left-brained accountant and later systems analyst, I believed that if I could solve a problem logically, that was all there was to it. The computer program or system, if properly tested, would produce the results expected—right? Wrong! What about people? What about cause and effect? What about feedback and learning? The design of the system and the reliability of the software were the tip of the iceberg. How people adapted and used the system, rather than being adapted (or programmed) by the system, made the difference between a solution that worked and one that didn't. (In fact, though, systems do change people as well as being changed by people.) Slowly, the reality that my worldview was incomplete dawned on me. There were other factors at work, indeed a new reality. That new reality, that understanding that everything is connected to everything else and that my ability to solve a problem by breaking it down into its components wasn't enough, made profound changes in this, the second half of my career. Systems Thinking principles guided me to a new way of thinking about all of my work, and in particular, a lifelong interest in why things work or don't work as I thought that they would or should.

I am not asking that you give up your present way of thinking, whatever that is. What I am asking is that you hold a different, additional view, at least for a while—a view that presents a model of cause and effect, feedback and learning—*a model that will enable us to anticipate, understand, and take action around the intended and unintended consequences of our choices and decisions.*

Models of Systems Thinking

Let's begin our discussion of a different model with two very conceptual illustrations of the two points of view. (See Figure 3.1.) In the mechanical, linear world of Newton, cause and effect were clear—"A" caused "B." In the Systems Thinking view, "A" may cause "B" as well as other outcomes not pictured. But that is not all. Systems Thinking teaches us that there may be a delay in space and time between the action caused by "A" and

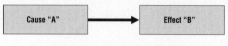

The Linear, Mechanical View

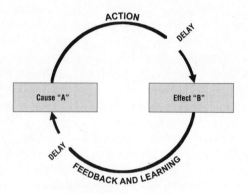

The Systems Thinking View

FIGURE 3.1   Two Points of View

the outcome of "B," and the outcome of "B" also provides feedback and learning for "A."

There is a very big difference in these views—a difference that helps to explain why things really happen the way they do.

Some Examples

Car sales are going down. Auto companies add promotions, rebates, zero financing. Car sales go up. Auto company profitability goes down. Rebates are pulled. Customers stop buying. The root cause of the decline in auto sales has not been addressed. The question of value, from a customer perspective, has not been answered.

The board of directors temporarily suspends the code of ethics at Enron. Executives take actions that are self-dealing and would be a violation were the previous ethics policies in force. The self-dealing transactions unwind and don't work anymore. Enron declares bankruptcy. The cause and effect in this case is quite clear and very direct. The basic values and culture are behind "what went wrong at Enron."[3]

An organization continually misses goals. Goals are lowered and still missed. After many years the company fails. Here the cause and effect are very far apart in space and time. The failure to challenge the status quo, to innovate, and to figure out new ways to serve the customer leads to the slippery slope of gradual decay.

During the 1980s in an environment of a declining market for traditional insurance, Prudential puts pressure on its life insurance agents to meet ever-increasing sales targets. Sales increase, but so do incidents of violations of published sales practices. Incidents of violations go unreported. Class-action lawsuits by consumers result in huge payments to policyholders.

In every example, cause and effect are clear; however, they occurred considerably apart in space and time. The Systems Thinking component of feedback and learning and the decision-making process that would have surfaced the intended and unintended consequences of available choices and decisions were absent or ignored.

Outcomes or results that come from our choices and decisions are what risk and reward are all about. However, the key that separates Systems Thinking from conventional wisdom and logic is the reality of the connections between all parties and the role of feedback and learning. The Governance Model and the System of Governance that we will introduce in Chapter 5 are all about a framework for decision making, feedback, and learning in an environment of uncertainty.

Let's Relate Systems Thinking to Decisions and Decision Making

Systems Thinking teaches us that the complexity in decision making is not just the possible direct connection between cause and effect but all of the variability brought about by the myriad of connections through which our decisions must pass. Our decisions, like the networks of the Internet, follow circuitous paths of near infinite variability. It is this reality that separates outcomes from the actions that created them. As we have seen, often the outcome is so far away in space and time from the source decision that the path between the two cannot be traced. This interconnectedness is one reason why things go wrong in times and places that come as complete surprises.

Systems Thinking also teaches us about the role of feedback and learning in the decision-making process. Choices and decisions are not just about cause and effect but also about the role that feedback and learning play in the improvement—or worsening—in the decision-making process. Feedback and learning are really a pair of consequences of our action or inaction. Feedback, as we shall see later, provides information, while learning transforms that information into the capability and competences which, in turn, improve the decision making throughout the enterprise.

Systems Thinking helps us to trace our potential decisions through the loops or networks of consequences, intended and unintended, *before* we launch a course of action. Feedback and learning tell us what kind of job we did in anticipating and understanding those potential consequences. If there is no feedback and no learning from *both* good and bad decisions and their outcomes, we are doomed to repeat the mistakes of the past on the one hand, and on the other hand to not recognize that the results of a "good" decision maybe only temporary—and they usually are.

What Is a "Good" Decision and What Is a "Bad" Decision?

As the economists would say, "It all depends. . . . " It all depends on the degree of uncertainty involved, the range of choices available and the decisions made from those choices, and how we process information and learn. Systems Thinking and our Governance Model help us to deal with all of these variables.

A good decision and a good outcome, first, result in the attainment of a maximum of intended consequences and a minimum of unintended consequences over time and throughout the Extended Enterprise. Bad decisions, therefore, lead to a minimum of intended consequences and a maximum of unintended consequences. As we get into the Governance Model in Chapter 5, we will introduce the complexity of decision making brought about by certainty or uncertainty of outcomes and the tools available to help deal with those uncertainties. Chapter 5 will introduce the Governance Model in detail; however, for the purposes of providing examples of Systems Thinking, I will organize those examples using the major components of the Governance Model:

- Strategy
- Execution
- Operations
- Organization, management process, and information

A Few More Specific Illustrations

At this point, I would like to illustrate some specific examples of how what appeared to be good decisions at a point in time actually created future problems that may or may not have been possible to anticipate at the time those decisions were made. The purpose of these illustrations is not to criticize the companies involved, but to recognize that most decisions must be scrutinized from the perspective of what may happen if the decision leads to a successful or an unsuccessful outcome.

Strategy   A product that is successful early in its life cycle is generally so profitable that an entire industry or company may be launched and become successful. How many of us remember that the original spread-sheet, Visicalc, launched Apple Computer? Cause and effect were at work. Competition from IBM and Microsoft was actually created by Visicalc. Could that competition have been anticipated, understood, and acted upon before the demise of Visicalc? We will never know; however, it would be interesting to know whether the strategic decisions of Apple anticipated and understood the potential consequences of the success of Visicalc.

In most successful product situations, over time competition is introduced; perhaps government funding is tightened, customer expectations shift, profitability declines. In this instance, the successful company, PacifiCare, is an $11.5 billion managed health care company based in Cypress, California. Overreliance for too long on one product, the Medicare health maintenance organization (HMO), nearly brought down the company. Was the decision to launch the Secure Horizons product in 1986 a "bad" decision? Of course not. From the range of choices available, it was a great decision, well executed. Then what went wrong? A failure to anticipate, understand, and take action around the consequences of the decision at the time the decision was made. Systems Thinking applied to this example might have played out the future reality that a highly profitable product not only attracts competitors, but in this case, prompts government action to reduce reimbursements. Continuing to grow Medicare revenue in the new reality of the Federal Balanced Budget Act of 1997 began a death spiral of continued erosion of margins. The Systems Thinking lesson here illustrates the reality that all success is temporary in the absence of continued innovation and change.

PacifiCare recovered from its death spiral under the leadership of Howard Phanstiel, a colleague and friend from my consulting days at Citicorp and as a fellow executive officer at WellPoint Health Networks. Howie's experience as an executive officer in several regulated public companies placed him in a unique position not only to understand what happened at PacifiCare but also to structure the decisions required to rejuvenate the company. PacifiCare, under Howie's leadership, made several of what I call "Big Decisions" at a strategic level not only to turn the company around but to assure its future success.

During an interview that I conducted with Howie in the course of researching examples for inclusion in this book, the Big Decisions were discussed, including the anticipation of the intended and unintended consequences of those decisions.

Strategic choices and decisions, which I have defined as governance, created a situation at PacifiCare that might have been avoided. Strategic choices and decisions also created a situation that provided PacifiCare with a new life.

As Howie related the PacifiCare story, the company was one of the early "delegated HMOs" built on a business model that was a win-win for health care providers, patients, and insurance payors. The staff model HMO, pioneered by Kaiser Permanente on the West Coast, helped to create an environment for what is now known as managed health care. Using a delegated network model HMO, PacifiCare, as an intermediary, contracted with doctors, hospitals, and others to provide whatever care was required to a specific set of customers, who would pay a fixed monthly premium. It was a win-win because the providers were guaranteed a set amount of revenue and predictable up-front cash flow, and the customers "free" access to health care services, including preventative care, without the hassle of filing claims for these services or of having to pay co-insurance. The intermediary, PacifiCare, made a profit by bringing the parties together, and largely avoided expense associated with actuarial, underwriting, medical management, and claims adjudication that plagued its competitors.

The business model worked so well that the federal government adopted it for Medicare patients in 1986. The program grew, in large measure because acceptance of managed care grew, particularly in the West. Medicare HMOs like PacifiCare were able to redeploy savings generated through managed care into richer benefit designs that made the HMO very attractive to seniors and their physicians. Being a Medicare HMO brought with it a set of unintended consequences, among which was the requirement that for each Medicare member enrolled, a commercial member had to be enrolled in the health plan. PacifiCare met this requirement by enrolling commercial members into equally rich benefit plans at very attractive prices. PacifiCare also missed the trend of the ever-growing popularity of the preferred provider organization (PPO) network model, which provides commercial members a wider choice of doctors and hospitals. The high margins on the Medicare business, for a time, disguised the inefficiencies and low margins of the commercial business, both for PacifiCare and its providers. Indeed, the margins were so attractive that PacifiCare embarked on a program of acquisition based on expansion of the Medicare business, which led to what amounted to imbalanced growth and concentration. PacifiCare's stock price nevertheless soared to the delight of the investment analysts, who saw a workable model for managing the double-digit growth of health care costs.

If you take an advance look at the figures later in the chapter showing the enterprise loop, the environment loop, and the enterprise and its environment, you will see that the uncontrolled growth of the enterprise met the controlling forces of the environment with the result of increased complexity, volatility, and risk to the PacifiCare organization. Specifically, the social forces of the failed Clinton administration health care task force, public outcry over the intrusiveness of managed care, the threat of *A Patient's Bill of Rights*, and a general sense that the federal government was paying too much in Medicare HMO reimbursements drove changes to public policy and regulation. Those changes, in turn, caused the competition as well as many of its providers, to exit the market and capital markets to challenge the formerly successful business model. Indeed, the 1997 Balanced Budget Act set out to reform the Medicare risk program through a new set of low-margin products and a commitment to take $40 billion out of the Medicare+Choice program over a five-year period.

PacifiCare was fundamentally a one-product company, and with eroding profit margins. Further, it lacked both the business model and core infrastructure to support full risk contracting and dedelegation of its network model. However, PacifiCare, like many successful companies, found it difficult to contemplate the changes in the culture and business model that would be required to compete on the new playing field.

Howard Phanstiel summarized the unintended consequences of the choices and decisions that characterized the enterprise:

- Overconcentration on a single product and single revenue source.
- Overreliance on a business model that was no longer sustainable.
- A perceived liquidity crisis.
- A crisis of leadership.
- Significant morale problems.

PacifiCare, when Howie came on board in 2000, faced an enormous turnaround challenge.

Howie and the PacifiCare board dealt with the reality of the enterprise and its environment and made the decisions required to transform the organization. With a limited availability of choices and a need to keep the ship afloat, the board and executive management decided to:

- Turn around each business unit of the company and earn their way out of the situation, rather than sell off their best assets in order to reduce debt.
- Leverage the company's Medicare+Choice business and its leading Secure Horizons brand into a new commercial senior business.
- Grow the company's specialty products as a core competency.
- Continuously develop new commercial products and indeed become a product leader within the industry.
- Use Medicare+Choice cash flow to reduce debt and provide resources for investments in the future.

In short, Howie and the board made a commitment to evolve from a Medicare HMO to a full-service managed care organization (MCO) and eventually a leading consumer health organization.

Perhaps as important to the future strategy of PacifiCare is the feedback and learning that will enable PacifiCare to continuously anticipate, understand, and take action around the consequences of its choices and decisions.

Execution   A major change initiative is introduced in order to execute a well-considered strategy. Indeed, as a part of the strategy decision, the need for a carefully considered change management effort was anticipated, understood, and acted upon. The change initiative, in the form of a major process redesign and reengineering effort, is launched. Tens of millions of dollars are spent on consultants, technology, and facilities. Organization change management experts are hired. However, the multiyear projects miss first-year milestones. The project is replanned. The new milestones are missed. The project is abandoned. The strategy does not get implemented. This is a familiar example. What went wrong? Was the strategic decision a bad decision? Taken as an isolated decision without considering the implications of execution, the strategic decision may have been sound. Was the execution approach wrong? Yes! Had the consequences of execution been thoroughly considered, the strategic decision may well have been flawed.

The point of the example is simply that strategy cannot be established without giving consideration to choices and decisions around execution and operations. Systems Thinking teaches us that the nearly infinite number of connections in such a massive endeavor introduces such complexity as to be nearly unmanageable. Systems Thinking also teaches us to look for leverage points in which relatively small efforts will produce huge gains. In this case, a series of small pilot projects would have demonstrated not only the effectiveness of the strategy, but also the effectiveness of the approach to execution. The original strategic thinking should have played out the intended and unintended consequences of various approaches (choices) to execution, but also to the eventual feedback and learning that would take place from both a possible poorly executed strategy and an effectively executed strategy. Is this a familiar story?

Operations   A well-executed strategy produces targeted operational results for several years. However, over time costs begin to increase, productivity declines, and quality erodes. What went wrong? Was the strategy flawed? Was execution improper? Was operational planning at fault? The answer to all three questions is no!—at least at the time the decisions were made and execution was undertaken. In a left-to-right linear world, we would continue to push harder on the operational organization to make it work. We would freeze or cut the budget, stop hiring, and so on. In a world of Systems Thinking, we would recognize the signs of obsolescence in our operational model. Instead of trying to drain the last ounce from what was once an effective set of activities and processes, we would recognize that a different set of activities and processes must be investigated. The feedback and learning from the results of our past choices and decisions would tell us that it is time to consider new choices and decisions. Perhaps consideration needs to be given to some form of outsourcing or partnerships; or perhaps our costs, under any circumstances, cannot be collected in our prices. The feedback and learning inherent in Systems Thinking might cause us to consider changing our value proposition—business model—or exiting the market.

Organization, Management Process, and Information Oxford Health Plans, Inc. was a hot HMO during the middle 1990s. Through an aggressive growth campaign, the then CEO, Stephen Wiggins, promised providers (hospitals and doctors) very favorable cost reimbursements compared to the competition. Oxford also promised companies and individuals very favorable prices compared to the competition for a wide range of covered services. Competitors asked, "How can this upstart company keep all of its promises?" The answer was, "We have a new model with none of the bureaucracy and costs of the old, traditional carriers." Oxford siphoned off the best customers of the traditional carriers, nearly causing the failures of many of them. Oxford then hit a wall. All of the unrestrained growth led to a backlog of unpaid physician and hospital bills, denial of services to customers, regulatory intervention, and failure.

What went wrong? The much-vaunted operational model didn't work, and nobody knew it until it was too late. Feedback and learning in the form of information and management process failed to inform management that its promises to customers and providers were too good to be true and an operational system designed for a much smaller company was inadequate for a large, fast growing company. Would a systemic perspective around cause and effect and the consequence of choices and decisions have made a difference? Only if the board and senior management could look at the world differently. The failure and eventual turnaround at Oxford provide an important lesson on the subject of governance and risk. This failure could have been anticipated using Systems Thinking. The turnaround by Dr. Norman Payson and his team was very well executed. Oxford is now a healthy, successful competitor in the metropolitan New York market.

I have tried in these pages to illustrate Systems Thinking concepts and compare them to our traditional ways of looking at decision making and risk. In traditional, linear thinking we "flog the product till it dies," as one client related to me. Or we "beat the fast horse," in the words of another. In other words, we keep doing what used to work—and what made us as individuals successful—until it doesn't work anymore. Systems Thinking teaches us to examine continuously cause and effect, and in particular to understand causes, while at the same time processing feedback from the environment and learning throughout the organization.

WHAT IS A SYSTEM?

First, let's discuss what a system is not. In the preceding chapter, we talked about conventional wisdom around *what* constitutes governance and risk—a list of outcomes or results that could be categorized into topics or pieces, and a fragmented structure for dealing with those pieces. A ball of twine might be made up of pieces of string of different lengths, texture, color, and so on, rolled up into a ball. That ball of twine is *not* a system of risks the enterprise must contemplate. That ball of twine is nothing but pieces of string wrapped around each other. You take a piece from the ball and you still have a ball of twine.

In contrast, a system consists of components that comprise a whole. You take away a component and the system no longer functions. Pieces of unrelated parts do not make a whole or a system. For example, weather systems: You take away a component such as wind and the system changes. The digestive system: You take away gastric juices and the system changes. Ecological systems: You take away the rain forest and the ecology of the region, if not the globe, changes.

What about commercial systems? Telecommunications systems depend on the interrelationships among an enormous number of pieces that must be put together before the first element of voice or data is communicated. The same is true of logistics systems, compensation systems, systems of change management, and so on. The important point is this: The pieces do not stand alone. There is little value to the pieces. It is only when the pieces come together into a whole that value is created. That is the idea behind the whole being greater than the sum of its parts.

Systems Thinking as applied to governance and risk illustrates what constitutes a system. The consequences, intended and unintended, of our choices and decisions across an Extended Enterprise, together with how we organize our decision-making processes to take advantage of the feedback and learning that takes place at all levels, constitute a system—a system of governance and risk.

The Structure of Systems

A system or network of pieces that comprise a system not only is intangible, it is a very abstract concept—a concept difficult to describe with words. How do we make the intangible tangible? How do we make the abstract concept of a system real and visible? The most helpful way I have found of answering these questions is through the use of diagrams of what are called feedback loops. Feedback loops illustrate cause and effect—circular relationships.

At the highest level of abstraction, and according to the theories of quantum mechanics, all of the parts of the universe are interconnected and react with each other in a causal way. For our purpose, we will come down to earth and consider feedback loops to explain cause and effect, and related consequences, at the level of the Extended Enterprise and its relationship to its environment. We really only need to get our minds around feedback loops and the structure of systems at the level at which we live. For a detailed explanation of the Extended Enterprise, you may wish to refer to Chapter 4 before going through this discussion of feedback loops.

At the level of the Extended Enterprise and its environment, our System of Governance is depicted and made visible by feedback loops that relate our enterprise to the environment in which it must function. Think of feedback and feedback loops as the transmission of information or signals that we must anticipate, understand, and take action upon.

There are two kinds of feedback or signals we need to understand in order to visualize how a system works: positive and negative. Positive feedback, depicted in our diagrams with a + sign, amplifies or reinforces a signal sent through a loop. Negative feedback, depicted by a – sign, dampens or places limits on a particular activity. As we will show by example, both types of feedback are necessary for an enterprise to grow on the one hand and to achieve a degree of stability on the other hand.

Examples of positive feedback loops include:

- *Audio feedback.* What is called feedback when a microphone is placed too near an amplifier? The resulting squawk is the result of the signal from the microphone being continuously amplified—potentially until ultimately the speaker blows out.
- *Compound interest buildup.* Each time interest is added to principal and amplified by another cycle, principal increases.

■ *Unrestricted revenue growth.* Organizations that reward sales growth as amplified by commissions and other behavioral motivators will grow until the enterprise destroys itself.

Examples of negative feedback loops include:

■ *A thermostat.* The setting of a thermostat at a predetermined temperature causes the heating or air-conditioning to switch on or off.
■ *A toilet float valve.* The water tank fills until the float valve shuts off the water supply.
■ *A budget.* Spending increases until constrained by predetermined limits.

Let's use a loop from each list to make an example. The positive loop, unrestricted growth, is constrained by the negative loop, a budget, in the form of prices and costs. The positive loop provides growth, while the negative loop provides stability. Both are necessary.

Now, let's illustrate the structure of a system with two feedback loops—one positive and the other negative—and how they come together.

The Extended Enterprise Loop

First, let's look at the enterprise loop—a positive (+) feedback loop (Figure 3.2).

FIGURE 3.2   The Enterprise Loop
Reprinted with permission from Deloitte & Touche LLP.

Where does the cycle begin? Some might say that everything begins with the customer. As Peter Drucker teaches, "The purpose of the corporation is to create a customer." Others might say that organizations are goal-oriented; therefore, setting growth and profitability targets is the beginning of the loop. I believe that great companies start with great people—people who have a vision of how the world might be a better place when their concept is successful.

Let's begin with the human organization. The knowledge and intellectual capital of the human organization create value for the markets and customers. Indeed, the human organization "creates" the customer. Moving along the loop, the value created for and by the customer creates the goal-oriented profitable growth that sustains the enterprise.

As feedback and learning take place, the human organization becomes more satisfied, more motivated; this in turn creates greater and greater customer satisfaction. Customers who perceive value and whose expectations are exceeded pay a premium in terms of prices; this, of course, enhances the profitability of the enterprise. The cycle, if left unchecked, would continue until something happened. A positive feedback loop, just as in the example of the speaker and the microphone, would blow up, or, as a physicist would say, it would enter a state of entropy or chaos, a state of disorder in what we are calling a closed system or feedback loop.

But something always happens before the system self-destructs. What happens is the impact of the external environment. As we said in the PacifiCare case, the company's growth and profitability went largely unchecked until the environment loop kicked in in the form of a reduction in Medicare reimbursement rates. Let's take a separate look at the environment.

The Environment Loop

The environment loop is a negative (–) feedback loop (see Figure 3.3). It is a system that provides stability, or some might say a brake on the uncontrolled, positive feedback loop of the Extended Enterprise.

There are at least three major loops associated with the environment. Each loop, of course, stands on its own as well as making connections with other loops:

1. Social forces
2. Public policy
3. Competition and capital markets

Social forces, including demographics, the environment, and consumer attitudes, all impact one another in ways with which we are all familiar.

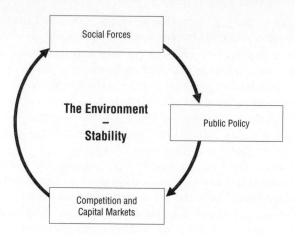

FIGURE 3.3 The Environment Loop
Reprinted with permission from Deloitte & Touche LLP.

The demographics of population growth (or lack thereof), income, and energy and food consumption all relate to public policy at global, national, and local levels. Public policy, in turn, presumably reflecting the will of the people, impacts legislation regulation and eventually economic growth (or lack thereof). As is the case with most drivers of change, social forces are often far distant in time and space from the public policy loops they create.

Competition and capital markets loops are combined into one subsystem of the environment loop because of the way in which they interact with each other. Competition and capital markets are "connected at the hip" with one another inasmuch as competition provides incentives and challenges for renewal, innovation, and growth, while the capital markets provide the intellectual and financial resources to feed that growth. Signals or information from new entrants to the markets served by the Extended Enterprise provide the feedback and learning required to anticipate, understand, and take action around the opportunities and risks that are presented. Signals from the capital markets provide information regarding the anticipated impact of changes in social forces, public policy, and competition.

Case Study: "What Happened to the Public Accounting Profession?"

A contemporary example of unintended consequences and a delay between public policy and its eventual impact is found in the public accounting profession—a body I have been associated with for nearly 40 years. The profession through the code of ethics of both national and state societies banned advertising, solicitation of each other's clients, and contingent fees. The standards of professional conduct, in effect, banned competition among what was then known as the Big Eight. If we look at the environment loop, that ban on competition provided stability and limited the growth of the individual firms—the enterprise loop.

In the 1970s, the Federal Trade Commission decided that the ban on advertising, solicitation, and contingent fees really represented anticompetitive practices and sued to force the professional association to lift such bans. Ultimately, with the exception of contingent fees, such restrictions were lifted after due warnings by leaders in the profession concerning the impact of unintended consequences. Among those anticipated but little understood consequences was the race for growth and heightened competition among the Big Eight.

Since the market for growth in traditional auditing and accounting services was limited by an ever-decreasing number of corporate entities, growth had to come from offering other professional services. The offering of nonauditing services evolved over the next 25 years to result in:

- Growth of services other than auditing and accounting such that these core activities eventually represented less than one-half of firm revenues.
- Increased use of the audit client base as a logical market in which to sell the additional services.
- Emergence of a public perception of a conflict of interest around the independence and objectivity of the professionals who performed the traditional public accounting services.

Despite the best efforts of the public accounting profession to show that independence and objectivity were not compromised and that indeed a broad range of services actually provided a broader perspective on the business of the enterprise, public policy debate that raged in the aftermath of major corporate scandals resulted in the Sarbanes-Oxley Act of 2002.

What went wrong? First, from a static, linear, cause-and-effect perspective, the Federal Trade Commission made the public accounting profession a competitive industry. The Big Eight, in a quest for growth, consolidated and became the Big Five. End of story—*almost*!

What actually happened, from the perspective of Systems Thinking, were the unintended consequences that played out over the next generation. The firms, which by state law had to be organized as partnerships and with unlimited personal liability, became huge, global enterprises. Management was, in some cases, diverted from the task of quality assurance to the management of growth, and the accounting and auditing services became a smaller and smaller percentage of a firm's total scope of services and revenue. Fueled by few constraints on lawsuits, frivolous or not, the enormous damage awards by juries resulted in liability insurance becoming unavailable at any price. The firms are now largely self-insured.

Following the boom of the 1990s and the inevitable market corrections, many of the excesses and, in some cases, illegal and unethical behavior and greed came home to roost. The price was high: eroded investor confidence. Who is to blame? In addition to boards of directors, some of whom were accomplices with management, the public accounting profession took the hit. From the dynamic, cause-and-effect world of feedback and learning and the unintended consequences of events of 30 years ago, the seeds of Sarbanes-Oxley and the Public Company Accounting Oversight Board (PCAOB) were sown. I doubt very much if the authors of the Act were even aware that they were dealing with a problem largely created by the Federal Trade Commission in the 1970s.

As of this writing, the Big Five is now the Big Four with Arthur Andersen as a firm taking the hit for Enron, and three of the remaining firms divesting themselves of their large systems consulting practices. I am not going to indulge myself in speculation on what will happen to what is left of a once valued profession given the potential consequences of greater regulation and a more risk-averse attitude on the part of the remaining firms.

I am relating this historic perspective on the public accounting profession, not in its defense, but to provide a rich example of "why things go wrong" and why our failure to anticipate, understand, and take action around the consequences of our choices and decisions is at the heart of Systems Thinking as applied to governance and risk.

The Enterprise and Its Environment

Figure 3.4 depicts how the enterprise and its environment join to create the reality of where we live.

The Extended Enterprise, with its potential for unchecked goal-driven enthusiasm and purpose, is brought back to earth or stabilized by the reality of the environment. The complexity, volatility, and risk that occur at the intersection of the two feedback loops presents the "white water" of opportunity and risk. Organizations that really understand and learn from how both the systems of the enterprise and the systems of the environment interact with one another are positioned to achieve above-average rewards for assuming average risks. The connection between risk and reward occurs right at the intersection of the two major systems. Those enterprises that really do anticipate, understand, and take action around the consequences of their choices and decisions will navigate the "white water" of opportunity and risk to achieve a sustainable competitive advantage.

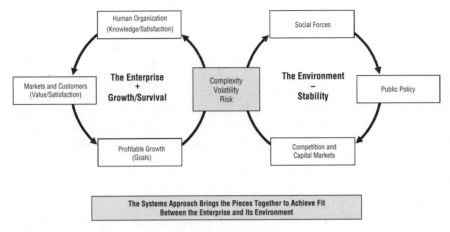

FIGURE 3.4   The Enterprise and Its Environment
Reprinted with permission from Deloitte & Touche LLP.

HOW DOES ALL OF THIS RELATE TO GOVERNANCE AND RISK?

I strongly believe that a working understanding of how Systems Thinking may be applied to the Extended Enterprise and its relationship to its environment is a prerequisite to:

- Understanding *what* risk really is.
- Figuring out *how* to organize decision making to minimize risk and maximize opportunity.

I also understand that boards of directors and senior executives do not spend their waking hours thinking about systems. That said, the perspective or point of view we are introducing will go a long way in educating boards and management around why things don't turn out the way we thought they would (i.e., why things go wrong) and what we might do about creating better outcomes. As we apply Systems Thinking to governance and risk in succeeding chapters, a knowledge of the implications of cause and effect and feedback and learning is a prerequisite.

CONCLUSION

All of this discussion about Systems Thinking and the connectivity of us all must lead somewhere. When clients ask what risks I feel their organizations face, my response is, "Show me your framework and process for decision making and I will tell you what risks you face." Clearly, I can't foretell the future any better than anyone else (and no one can). However, if an organization contemplates the future in terms of choices and decisions as opposed to relying on the vagaries of chance and luck, the outcomes are much less in doubt. Remember, the problem we defined and set out to solve in Chapter 2 was a failure to anticipate, understand, and take action around the intended and unintended consequences of our choices and decisions. I believe that Systems Thinking provides both the framework and process for dealing with that problem.

NOTES

1. Daniel H. Kim, *Introduction to Systems Thinking* (Waltham, MA: Pegasus Communications, 1999).
2. Peter M. Senge, *The Fifth Discipline* (New York: Doubleday, 1990).
3. Peter C. Fusaro and Ross M. Miller, *What Went Wrong at Enron* (Hoboken, NJ: John Wiley & Sons, 2002).

CHAPTER 4

The Extended Enterprise: We Are All Connected

INTRODUCTION

Today's world of networks, global relationships, and instantaneous communications has led us to what I have come to call "zero time, zero space, and zero slack." Cause and effect may still be separated by time and space, but the boundaries that once existed between and among organizations and their legal entities are gone. One only needs to look at systems of supply chain management and just-in-time logistics for examples of this reality.

My colleagues and I have come to call this reality the Extended Enterprise. Enterprises have always been extended with regard to suppliers, customers, regulators, and shareholders and other stakeholders, but never to the extent that we experience today and will experience tomorrow. Global alliances and the concept of outsourcing have led today's enterprises to extend themselves in ways we didn't think possible only a decade ago. Most organizations do business today with enterprises they don't even know. The implications of the Extended Enterprise on the subject of governance and risk are enormous. Decision making and the related intended and unintended consequences of those decisions presents a dilemma of nearly limitless proportions.

The concept of the Extended Enterprise will be continuously referred to throughout the remainder of this book as a constant reminder to boards and executive management that "every ship does not sail on its own bottom." The issues of governance and risk are more often encountered within the context of the Extended Enterprise than within the legal boundaries of the enterprise itself. The Governance Model introduced in the next chapter continues to reinforce this concept.

WHAT IS THE EXTENDED ENTERPRISE?

The days of organizations being vertically integrated such as we found in the automobile and even the computer industries are gone—at least for now. Henry Ford's River Rouge automobile plant in Detroit completed cars in one place from deliveries of sand and iron ore. The IBM of Tom Watson's day created everything it took to build a product from start to finish, largely in one location. In many ways, however, our perspectives and processes are still embedded with the notion that we are in control of our environment and our enterprise. Nothing could be further from the truth when we consider what kind of external relationships comprise our Extended Enterprise:

- Owners-investors and the public.
- Customers—including customers-to-be.
- Suppliers and counterparties.
- Competitors—existing and emerging.
- Regulators and rating agencies.
- Network partners.

This list of relationships comprises a more detailed version of the environment loop shown in Figure 3.3 in the preceding chapter. The environment loop is a negative (−) feedback loop. That is, the participants in our Extended Enterprise tend to put a damper on what might be the uncontrolled growth of the enterprise loop. We will discuss each participant in the Extended Enterprise separately; however, there are some overarching decisions to be considered regarding the Extended Enterprise as a whole.

BIG DECISIONS

The board and executive management must decide to embrace the concept of the Extended Enterprise and understand:

- The implications of governance and risk on the Extended Enterprise.
- That none of the participants in the Extended Enterprise may be ignored.
- That the value chain of the enterprise always contains participants of the Extended Enterprise.

In summary, the message for the board and executive management is simply this: The participants in the Extended Enterprise are powerful forces whose activities must be continuously anticipated, understood, and acted upon within the governance and decision-making processes of the enterprise. Said another way, failure to anticipate, understand, and take action around the consequences of choices and decisions relating to the Extended Enterprise has created many of today's notable crises of governance and risk.

PLAYERS IN THE EXTENDED ENTERPRISE

The Extended Enterprise includes participants that have long histories with the enterprise itself such as customers and suppliers. Indeed, some vertically organized enterprises in many industries (e.g., automotive, aerospace and defense, retailing and distribution) divested themselves of wholly owned subsidiaries, which in turn became members of an Extended Enterprise. Other members of the Extended Enterprise have emerged with new, stronger voices, such as owners and investing public, while still others have come about directly as a result of e-commerce and the Internet. Regardless of the origin of the players in the Extended Enterprise, corporate legal-entity walls have come down and the consequences of a much more fluid, organic organization must be anticipated, understood, and acted upon.

Owners—Investors and the Public

The Extended Enterprise recognizes the role of owners, whether they are share owners (including institutional investors), debt holders, policy owners, or the public in the case of not-for-profit or other public benefit corporations. The Extended Enterprise includes a constituency that must be an integral part of the governance of the enterprise. Decision making within the enterprise that does not contemplate the perspectives of the owners will ultimately produce an outcome that will threaten the survival and growth of the enterprise. Most of the literature on the subject of corporate governance underscores this issue by making the interests of the owners the number one priority of the board of directors. I certainly agree with the many voices on the subject, with one additional caveat—that the management representatives on the board share this responsibility to owners along with the independent directors. The board, as an agency for the owners, has a fiduciary responsibility not to be divided on this issue of representation. As we discussed earlier, the board has a fiduciary responsibility that goes far beyond the owners to a large community of stakeholders.

The decision-making role of the board and executive management must include a commitment to understanding the expectations of the owners as well as the imperative to develop and maintain open, two-way communications with those owners. Good governance, from my point of view, begins with a concerted effort on the part of the board and executive management to maintain open, continuous communication with their owners, whoever they may be.

Speaking of whoever they may be, the disconnect between the interests of the institutional investors and the individuals who own shares in mutual funds or whose pensions are managed by institutions comes to mind. When I interviewed Gerald Rosenfeld, CEO of Rothschild North America, Inc. on the subject of owners, he introduced the idea of real or beneficial owners as contrasted to investment managers. Gerry used the term "asymmetry of risk" to drive home the point of difference between the two stakeholders. Asymmetry of risk means, of course, that the real or beneficial owners actually experience greater risks than the investment managers who are measured and rewarded on a much shorter cycle—quarterly and annually. It is Gerry's sense that the time frames for investment managers be lengthened to more closely approximate the duration of the real owners' time frames. Boards, in particular, can take a leadership role in closing this disparity gap as they communicate with both constituencies and as they work with management in their dealings with analysts and buy-side investors.

Another perspective regarding owners relates not only to the actual holders of beneficial shares, most of who are no longer the original risk takers, but to the broader community of stakeholders. For boards and management to avoid what I believe is a short-term trap of attempting to manage to capital, the broader perspective of ownership may actually produce better returns over the long run.

Customers—Including Customers-to-Be

Chapter 3 introduced the role of markets and customers as an element of the enterprise loop. (See Figure 3.2.) The focus of the enterprise must be directed outward to the markets and customers. Depicting the markets and customers as an integral part of the enterprise loop provides a focus on value creation. Including the customers and the customers-to-be as a part of the Extended Enterprise also provides an outside-in focus. When you consider the fact that even those organizations with a huge share of market serve only a relatively small number of total customers in the market, the role of the customer-to-be is an important element of the Extended Enterprise. Most of our potential customers belong to our competitors.

The board and executive management, through the strategic planning processes to be discussed in succeeding chapters, make purposeful decisions around which markets and customers the organization will serve and how the enterprise will create value for those customers. The choices available and the decisions to be made from among those choices determine to a large extent the nature of the enterprise. The Extended Enterprise, including the customers and the customers-to-be, cannot be thought of separately from the enterprise itself. The strategic, careful, and thoughtful selection of customers is a decision-making and therefore governance and risk issue of the highest order.

An Example Travelers on Southwest Airlines expect to have a pleasant experience. Southwest personnel are screened to ensure that they enjoy people. Even business travelers get into the swing of things when they travel on Southwest. So what? From a governance and risk perspective, the customers of the Extended Enterprise are treated very much as a part of the enterprise itself. Were Southwest, for whatever reason, to begin to change the culture of the organization, it would lose the unique relationship it enjoys with its customers.

Another Example In this case, a professional services firm became quite successful by serving midlevel corporate managers through a staffing model that recruited professionals who could and did relate directly with their midlevel clients. A change was contemplated in the staffing model to recruit a more elite group of professionals who could market services to higher-level executives in the same client organizations the firm currently served. During a board strategy session with executive management, the consequences of the decision to move upscale were thoroughly discussed. It was finally determined that the consequences (i.e., the risks) of such a decision would significantly alienate both the existing client midlevel managers and the firm's professional staff. There was also the potential consequence that the strategy would not work because the senior executives of the potential client organizations were already being served by other professionals. The board and executive management considered the proposed decision to have "lose-lose" consequences.

While the two examples could be classified as strategy market segment issues, the point to be made in the context of the Extended Enterprise is that the customers and customers-to-be are "joined at the hip" with the corporate entity. Any choice or decision considered without deep reflection on unintended consequences will produce outcomes—risks—that threaten the survival of the organization.

Suppliers and Counterparties

Nowhere within the Extended Enterprise are the risks greater than in the selection and monitoring of relationships with the enterprises that create value for the customers of the organization itself. The choices and decisions that emanate from what amounts to the outsourcing of activities in the value chain or in the laying off of financial risks may produce immediate and often disastrous consequences. Every activity performed by an enterprise is subject to the risk that a third party in the Extended Enterprise will fail to perform or will perform in such a way as to jeopardize the survival of the parent organization. Governance and risk issues at all levels of the enterprise come into play when contemplating with whom we choose to do business.

A Prime Example   The aerospace and defense and automobile industries provide rich examples of supplier and counterparty relationships that work very well most of the time and are quite visible when they fail to work. These industries are no longer vertically integrated, but they are globally integrated. Parts and assemblies for aircraft and automobiles are fabricated all over the world and brought together for final assembly near the markets for which they are destined. Communications and integrated logistics make such relationships work most of the time. Not only do failures of communications bring about logistical nightmares and destroy the added values of just-in-time inventory systems, but failures of communications and the sharing of vital information between suppliers and counterparties may also prevent life-threatening consequences, particularly in the aerospace and defense and automobile industries.

For example, a failure of a part detected in one part of the network of suppliers may have disastrous consequences in another part of the network if not anticipated and acted upon in a timely manner. Further, from the perspective of Systems Thinking, cause and effect may be far apart in time and space. A seemingly small incident at one point in a process may have disastrous consequences at a different point and time. Current events that describe various disasters and product recalls make the point.

Suppliers are an integral part of the value creation activities of the Extended Enterprise. The board, together with executive, senior, and operating management must:

■ Know suppliers and counterparties well, including credit ratings.
■ Include suppliers and counterparties in the feedback loops of the Extended Enterprise.
■ Ensure that such feedback is used and that organizational learning is taking place.

A perspective on suppliers and counterparties that I have found helpful is to encourage them to be treated as customers rather than as vendors. By focusing on and understanding the needs, wants, and expectations of suppliers and assuring that the Extended Enterprise is practicing the principles of Systems Thinking, a positive relationship of mutual trust and respect is fostered. From a governance and risk perspective, decisions that foster close, cooperative relationships with suppliers of all types help the board and executive management to anticipate, understand, and, if appropriate, take action around the consequences of supplier decisions.

In another situation with which I am familiar, a large, innovative financial services organization marketed and sold a product manufactured by another company to its own customers. The creditworthiness of the company to which the product was outsourced came into question and its securities ratings were lowered. The customers who bought the product had redemption rights, which they exercised, causing immediate liquidity problems for the company that sold the product. The bottom line for the large financial services company was an intervention by regulators and a forced sale of the company. The full and potential impact of the counterparty risk was knowable by the board and executive management, but not anticipated, much less understood.

Competitors—Existing and Emerging

As pointed out in Chapter 3, the impact of competition and the behavior of competitors presents powerful environment loop forces on the organization (Figure 3.3). An outward-focused board and executive management are continuously facing choices, decisions, and consequences, particularly around emerging competitors. In today's networked world, to complicate matters even more, many of our competitors are our customers, suppliers, and network partners. It is through this maze of interconnected relationships that boards and executives must carefully steer a decision-making course.

Most organizations track their known, existing competitors pretty well, at least those organizations that are outwardly focused. Field forces are constantly encountering competitors in the lobbies or living rooms of their clients or customers. Systems Thinking teaches us that the feedback and learning that should take place as a result of those encounters are critical to anticipating, understanding, and taking action around the threats of existing competitors. How many boards and members of executive management listen and learn from such field input is truly a governance and risk issue. In my experience, the subject of competition is not an item on the agendas of most board meetings. The subject of emerging competitors is not on the agendas of most executive management meetings.

The major competition issue, from my point of view, is that of the emerging competitors. Most organizations never see them coming—because they are not looking. Yet it is the emerging competition that usually presents the greatest challenge and risk. Just ask the U.S. automotive companies about the threat of the Japanese in the 1960s. Or ask the big U.S. retailers about the threat of Wal-Mart and Home Depot in the 1970s. The Extended Enterprise view of most major organizations is full of examples of the new competitors that disrupt the status quo.

From a governance and risk standpoint, the role of existing and emerging competitors presents major threats and opportunities to the enterprise:

- Establishing prices
- Changing the value proposition

Existing competitors offer relatively little differentiation within established industries; thus the prices and value propositions reflect a status quo. Most existing competitors look much alike strategically; therefore, the threats are pretty well known. Most large, mature organizations have so much trouble creating change and differentiating themselves that boards and executive management may track their performance relatively easily, if they try.

Emerging competitors, in contrast, differentiate themselves quite well, and are able to disrupt both prices and the value proposition. These are the competitors that boards and executive management must be scanning the External Environment to anticipate, understand, and to take action in their regard. Emerging competitors are the real threat. How the board and executive management take action is a strategic decision, which will be discussed in Chapter 6. For now, as a part of our discussion around the Extended Enterprise, emerging competitors must at least be on the radar screen.

Regulators and Rating Agencies

First, let me reiterate a first principle—governance does not mean compliance. Governance, in part, means that decisions must be taken in order to be compliant. There is a big difference between these two points of view. This discussion of the Extended Enterprise and the decision-making roles of boards and executive management will assume that good governance is also a compliant governance, but the discussion doesn't end there.

The environment loop (Figure 3.3) shows public policy in the form of regulation being driven by social forces. As is often the case, social forces take shape long before the intervention of regulators. Such a lag in the cycle results in the acts of regulators being "behind the curve," implementing regulations whose time has passed or, worse still, putting in place regulations whose cure is worse than the illness. Nevertheless, the law is the law and we are a country of laws. The best way to change regulation, or at least to have a strong voice on regulation, is to influence the social forces in the first place. Board and executive management, often acting through industry associations, can do just that. Witness the Health Insurance Industry Association's Harry and Louise program launched in the early 1990s, which defeated the Clinton administration health care plan.

Given our previous discussion around Tone at the Top and being a compliant enterprise, the first-level decision around governance and risk is to assure that the enterprise, from top to bottom, does not wink at regulation. In my experience, when executive management attempts to ignore the spirit of regulation and to continuously look for loopholes, that message is sent throughout the enterprise and is amplified many times over. Noncompliant behavior becomes the Tone at the Top.

Having worked on a number of financial institutions that were under close regulatory supervision in the 1980s and 1990s, I came to observe the behavior of regulators who either had been lied to directly or in some other way felt deceived. The prevalent attitude, as you might expect, was one of anger, betrayal, and vengeance. The enterprises I observed did not have to fail. It was not inevitable that they would fail and be subject to some form of regulatory supervision. These organizations did not fail as a result of bad regulations, inept regulators, or poor oversight parties. These organizations failed as a result of bad decisions at the board and executive management levels—cases of bad governance.

I have observed organizations that in their quest for complaint behavior and in their efforts to please their regulators and rating agencies make management decisions that are detrimental to the enterprise. Governance and risk—decisions and consequences—must be carefully considered by boards and executive management before issues of survival and growth give way to a compliant but dying enterprise. The regulators have stakeholders—politicians and the public—who are not necessarily the constituencies charged with the long-term well-being of the enterprise.

It is up to the board and executive management to communicate a balanced view of the enterprise to all stakeholders, in particular regulators and rating agencies. The decision to present the enterprise first as compliant, and then from a fiduciary point of view concerned with the long-term economic health is an important one. One view, the regulatory view, is not sufficient to convey strategies of profitable growth.

In summary, the Extended Enterprise and the roles of regulators and rating agencies must be viewed from a governance and risk perspective in terms of compliance, not defiance, and in terms of open, trusting communications. Boards and executive management, through the Tone at the Top set the standard for the rest of the enterprise.

Network Partners

Today's Extended Enterprise is a node in a vast global network. We are all connected. We are all connected to and through partners we do not know. Our enterprises are at risk from sources we can barely imagine. How should the board and executive management make decisions in view of this enormous uncertainty? The answer, of course, is "very carefully." But beyond being aware of the uncertainties that result from dealing with the unknown, what frame of reference would be helpful? The Governance Model outlined in Chapter 5 establishes the required framework from strategy through operations. The issue here is to create a sense of anticipation and understanding that our enterprise is connected in its environment in ways that we may be able to barely comprehend. The Governance Model provides a framework for providing a best effort to achieve such comprehension under varying degrees of uncertainty.

An Example   Many organizations in today's world compete with their customers, suppliers, and other network partners. Until recently, few, if any, companies competed with their own customers. Today there are so many conflicting or potentially conflicting relationships that routine checks of conflicts reveal that most enterprises, in one way or another, are in conflict with every other enterprise. Organizations that find themselves in potential conflict situations cannot simply state that they will not do business in any situations that might present a potential conflict. There would be no one left with whom to do business. The decision-making process in such situations must begin with what I call the "test of the market." I don't personally believe that checklists or other compliance procedures can substitute for market-based transactions between members of the Extended Enterprise. If we all understood potential and actual exposure, decisions would have to be made at arm's length and based on market forces. For example, most Extended Enterprises depend on ever-expanding networks of customers, suppliers, and competitors to be effective. Policies established at the board and executive management levels and placed on the web site of the enterprise may display for all to view the firm's position regarding market-based relationships.

What about Other Network Partners?   Most, if not all, Extended Enterprises depend on network partners that are shared nationally, if not globally, including:

- The U.S. Postal Service.
- Telecommunications and other public utilities, such as energy and water.
- Software providers.

- Banks, particularly for funds transfer services.
- Transportation, including package delivery services.
- Internet service providers.
- Health care providers.
- Database providers, such as medical records and credit bureaus.
- Security services.

These network partners avoid being classified as customers, competitors, or suppliers. Network partners play an often invisible but critical role in the delivery of services without necessarily being a part of the service itself. Apart from being sensitive to the costs of the services, many enterprises do not take the failure or lack of availability of such services into their decision-making processes, particularly at a strategic level. For example, the anthrax threat to the U.S. Postal Service following the terrorist attacks of 9/11 presented enormous strategic challenges to direct mail organizations.

The complexity of today's interconnected world extends the framework of the Extended Enterprise and the intricate web of dependencies far beyond most views of decision making. Again, I think that the Governance Model presents a framework for considering varying levels of uncertainty around such decision making.

CONCLUSION

The Extended Enterprise is a reality of the global economy. We are all connected. The drivers of the global economy—from technology and the Internet to the economics of self-interest—have created enterprises of such complexity as to be barely understandable. Yet, from a governance and risk perspective, understand them we must. Each of the parties of the Extended Enterprise must be anticipated and understood as critical elements in the decision-making processes that will begin to unfold with the Governance Model introduced and discussed in the succeeding chapters. In particular, the Extended Enterprise must become the domain of the board and executive management. As we will see, the signals that portray change occur at the intersection of the Extended Enterprise and its environment and must be anticipated, understood, and acted upon.

PART TWO

Establishing a
New Perspective

The Governance Model and the System of Governance

INTRODUCTION

During the course of my journey, Systems Thinking provided the scientific basis for what my colleagues and I began to refer to as the Governance Model and the System of Governance. True to the philosophy of Systems Thinking, both models started with our thinking about the whole before the parts as well as the relationship between the two concepts.

Both the Governance Model and the System of Governance trace their roots back to the definitions of governance and risk and how both concepts converged during the journey:

- Governance is about decision-making from among available choices.
- Risk is the anticipation, understanding, and action around the consequences of those decisions.

As I considered the problem outlined in Chapter 2, "A Current Perspective: Why Things Go Wrong," I realized that to only establish a couple of definitions and to declare that Systems Thinking would provide the new perspective was far from an adequate milestone along the journey. What was really required, as I indicated in Chapter 1, was a sufficiently detailed framework and process that boards and senior executives could use as a guide.

The Governance Model and the System of Governance as they are introduced in this chapter and then detailed in subsequent chapters provide both framework and process.

WHAT THE GOVERNANCE MODEL AND
SYSTEM OF GOVERNANCE ARE NOT

The framework and process introduced in this chapter are designed to deal with decisions and related outcomes in the context of the enterprise (Figure 3.4) and the environment (Figure 3.3). Those two loops are dynamic. They operate in real time. Therefore, any system or approach that either is static or is "bolted on" to other systems of management will do little in terms of dealing with real risks.

The development and operation of a framework and process are not matters that may be delegated to the legal department, the chief financial officer (CFO), the chief risk officer (CRO), or any other corporate activity and checked off as meeting some regulatory or board requirement for corporate governance. The framework and process will not work if they are not the primary vehicle for decision making, receiving feedback, and learning.

Finally, referring to our first principle of Systems Thinking, the subsystems of the Governance Model and the System of Governance do not work if they are not considered as the whole. The pieces taken separately and without the connections to other subsystems will not work.

THE GOVERNANCE MODEL AND
THE SYSTEM OF GOVERNANCE

The Governance Model—shown in Figure 5.1—is a *noun*. The Governance Model is a framework and process, including the activities, tools, and methodologies that may be described, documented, taught, and put in place. The Governance Model is the decision-making framework and process designed to enable the Extended Enterprise to survive and grow within its environment. However, the Governance Model is just a framework and process—a noun—that is inert in the absence of a verb.

The System of Governance functions as a *verb*. The System of Governance is the active involvement of the board, executive management, indeed the entire enterprise in the dynamic, real-time operation of the Governance Model. Unfortunately, as with any system found in nature, the System of Governance is invisible. Yet it is the System of Governance that enables the subsystems of the Governance Model itself to work. The System of Governance will not work without the Governance Model. Said another way, the System of Governance is defined by how people work together to anticipate, understand, and take action around the consequences of their choices and decisions. Chapter 10, "Making It

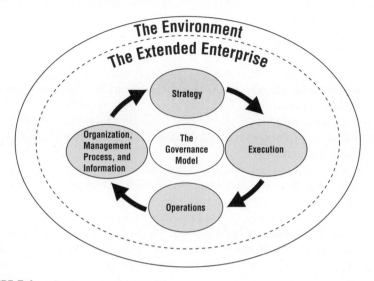

FIGURE 5.1 The Governance Model
Adapted from a diagram and reprinted with permission from Deloitte & Touche LLP.

Happen," addresses in considerable detail the use of the Governance Model for implementing the changes required to make the System of Governance work. This use of the Governance Model as an implementation framework was one of the lessons learned during the journey as well as the basis for the WellPoint Health Networks, Physicians Mutual Insurance Company, and Washington Mutual cases illustrated in Chapter 1.

My point is this: Boards and senior executives are being basically forced to *do something—anything* to deal with governance and risk. What to do must be chosen from a wide variety of topics, tools, methodologies, frameworks, and processes, all of which may deal with a piece of the problem and none may have to do with what I believe to be the real issue—the ability of the board and all levels of management to anticipate, understand, and take action around the consequences of their choices and decisions. The Governance Model, with its attendant process for implementation, is intended to provide guidance to the question of what to do. The Governance Model presents choices, decisions, feedback, and learning in a framework that deals with uncertainty and the white water of complexity, risk, and volatility that occur at the intersection of the enterprise and its environment.

THE SYSTEM OF GOVERNANCE

The Governance Model is a left-brain, logical framework for decision making. The Governance Model has no life or operational reality without the System of Governance. The Governance Model is a framework resting in a three-ring binder without the means of implementation.

As indicated previously, the System of Governance is a right-brain activity that enables the Governance Model to operate. One system cannot function without the other.

Even though I cannot reduce the System of Governance to a logical set of subsystems and related feedback loops, it is still possible to discuss the behavioral model for effective decision making. My comments are not designed to be a tutorial on leadership—there is an established body of knowledge on the subject of leadership. Rather, based on my consulting experience as well as on the interviews I conducted during my journey, I arrived at some examples of behavioral models that I believe lead to effective decisions.

I briefly described the contribution of Martha Clark Goss when I introduced Tone at the Top in Chapter 1. Tone at the top is the cornerstone of the System of Governance. Without the ethics-focused culture reinforced every day by the leadership of the enterprise, the organization is adrift and any old behavior is acceptable. To briefly summarize Martha's point of view:

> *People look to their leaders for cues as to what's acceptable and what isn't—notwithstanding what written policies may say. Leaders create culture.*
>
> *Examples set by CEOs as well as senior government officials encouraged pushing the envelope, breaking the rules.*
>
> *Punishments for breaking the rules were limited—companies were fined, but there was little impact on those responsible.*

The tone at the top of those enterprises that made headlines in 2001 to 2002 was clearly the driver of those failures. From a Systems Thinking perspective, the tone at the top characterized the System of Governance. The decisions, conscious or not, made by boards and executive management led to the outcomes that we have all witnessed. The feedback and learning that took place reinforced the notion that the behavior of the leadership not only was appropriate, it was the preferred way of doing business.

Dialogue

The most successful organizations I know adopt a style that fosters dialogue and open communications and learning throughout the subsystems of the Governance Model. Board members or senior executives who listen carefully, protect the views of others, and make certain that all ideas—in particular, the consequences of ideas—are fully explored end up making better decisions. In contrast, senior executives who, by dint of their position, feel compelled to know everything invariably become the limiting factor in the decision-making process. In other words, the power of position limits the ability of the organization to completely explore the consequences of choices and decisions. Even worse, the use of power in the decision-making process prohibits organizational learning from taking place. Mistakes of the past tend to be repeated, and the underlying causes of successes are not well understood.

During the course of my journey, I interviewed Julie Hill several times. Julie is a civic leader, member of the board of directors of Well-Point Health Networks, and member of the boards or past president of a number of philanthropic organizations. Julie also served as CEO of Costain Homes, a U.K.-based home builder. My objective in discussing governance and risk with Julie was, of course, to learn from her experiences in both the public and private sectors as well as to understand her points of view as a CEO and as a director of a public company. Many of Julie's comments are incorporated throughout this book in terms of roles and responsibilities of board members and CEOs. Julie, however, brought another point of view, one that I am including here under the heading of "Dialogue."

Julie's point of view had to do with the relationship between dialogue and diversity. It is Julie's belief, backed up by research conducted by the Conference Board of Canada, that diversity not only facilitates dialogue and learning among board members, but it also is highly correlated with organizational performance and profitability. In the research conducted by the Conference Board of Canada, the appointment of women to boards served as a proxy for diversity. Indeed, having a critical mass of women sitting on a particular board created a greater opportunity to consider different points of view and perspectives. Given that the thesis of this book rests on the adoption of a different perspective on governance and risk, Julie's input is most useful and appropriate.

Dialogue as a management style does not come easily to most organizations and senior executives. It is a learned skill that is acquired only in an atmosphere and environment of trust and mutual respect. The organizations that I have encountered over my career that have mastered dialogue as a management style create a deep bench of competent executives. Conversely, the hierarchical chain of command and power structures create marginal organizations that never focus on anything but personal success; effective decision making at the senior executive level is limited to the competencies of primarily one person.

Long-Term Thinking

Survival and growth are not quarterly phenomena. A focus on quarterly earnings and the continued threat of stock market retribution for missed numbers haunt most senior executives and boards. The fear of class-action lawsuits being brought by lawyers whose computer systems constantly track stock prices is both real and irrational. The decision-making processes that are inherent in the Governance Model have no place for producing a known outcome every 90 days. Indeed, pressure for short-term earnings when coupled with an incentive compensation system that rewards short-term behavior is a huge obstacle to survival and long-term growth. Indeed, the time frame for decision making, including the consideration of the consequences of decisions, is limited to a quarter, or at most a year. Many CEOs simply hope that nothing bad happens on their watch. I don't believe that short-term thinking, reward systems, and shortened tenure of CEOs are coincidences.

I understand, having worked for a public company and having sat on the boards of two other public companies, the pressures placed on CEOs and CFOs from investment analysts with their own models and their own agendas for quarterly and annual results. The short-term pressures bring about both short- and long-term consequences that are devastating to any model that attempts to apply the concepts of governance and risk. I am, however, encouraged by recent pronouncements from prominent public companies that indicate they will no longer provide quarterly earnings guidance. This is a step in the right direction.

Governance and risk suffer at both the board and senior executive levels because decisions are taken that produce outcomes that are not consistent with the long-term growth and survival of the enterprise. Among the most notorious decisions associated with bad governance are the strategies to merge or acquire in the name of growth and accretive earnings. Growth by merger or acquisition merely puts two entities together that were not meeting analysts' expectations and attempts to achieve so-called synergies through reductions in the workforce. Most mergers and acquisitions do not achieve targeted long-term objectives, but the board and executive management are given short-term credit for a forward-thinking strategy. The investment bankers and lawyers benefit more often than the shareholders.

The System of Governance will work effectively with the Governance Model only to the degree that the logical framework of the Governance Model is enabled by a compatible behavioral model. To the extent that the rewards produced by the Governance Model are incompatible with the desired behavior of the System of Governance, the long-term outcomes of survival and growth will not be achieved. For example, excessive CEO compensation, particularly when not reflective of corporate performance, will destroy the firm's ability to establish dialogue among the board and senior executives and to communicate a long-term perspective to employees, share owners, and other stakeholders.

Incentive Compensation

The systems of compensation will drive behavior one way or the other. The intended and unintended consequences of the systems of compensation will either facilitate the growth and survival of the enterprise or destroy the enterprise. One of the key behavioral linkages between the System of Governance and the Governance Model is the linkage between the objectives of the enterprise and the design of incentives also developed within the strategy subsystem. Incentive compensation systems that pay out when corporate objectives are achieved create behaviors within the System of Governance that enable the Governance Model to work. Incentive compensation—in particular, CEO compensation packages that do not relate to corporate objectives—destroy any efforts to achieve effective governance and to assure long-term growth and survival. Indeed, to quote Peter Drucker once again, as the pay gap increases between the CEO and the general employee population, it will make a mockery of the contributions of all the other employees in a successful organization.

Summary of Behavioral Characteristics of the System of Governance

The combined behavioral impact of dialogue, long-term thinking, and incentive compensation systems define the behavioral modeling of the enterprise. Firms that talk, listen, and learn together; that apply Systems Thinking to the long-term consequences of their choices and decisions; and that pay for performance create great sustainable enterprises. Those that don't, don't.

SUBSYSTEMS OF THE GOVERNANCE MODEL

The four major subsystems of the Governance Model present, in a systemic way, a framework for evaluating choices, making decisions, and processing the feedback and learning that result from those choices and decisions throughout the Extended Enterprise. Each subsystem links to each other subsystem in an effort to track consequences through all levels of the enterprise. Each subsystem will be introduced here and then expanded in subsequent chapters.

Drilling Down into the Governance Model—Big Picture

Figure 5.2 describes, in greater depth, the four subsystems of the Governance Model and the linkages between each level. The subsystems will be described in the following four chapters: however, you can follow the logic of each chapter by viewing the manner in which choices and decisions are considered by level of organization and the nature of those choices and decisions from strategy to operations and on through organization, management process, and information. Figure 5.2 appears to be static, that is, locked into time horizons and a planning calendar. The reality is, I do not know how to draw a diagram of a dynamic model. As I reviewed Figure 5.2 with Bill Longbrake at Washington Mutual, Bill added the helpful point that the model is really continuously being adapted to changes in circumstances. Senior executives at Washington Mutual are constantly scanning the environment and making strategic decisions to achieve a fit with that environment.

Strategy—Outcomes Associated with the Future   Strategy for the purposes of this illustration is depicted as a corporate activity conducted by the relatively few board and senior executives who come together to plan the future of the enterprise over a three- to five-year period. Organizations such as General Electric, General Motors, and huge energy companies that comprise multiple business models will undoubtedly make strategic decisions at a division or strategic business unit level. The logic remains the same, however, with the nature of the choices and decisions occurring at a division level rather than at the corporate level. The decisions made at the strategy level flow to the execution or business unit level as inputs to the assessment activity, which occurs at that level. The decisions made at the strategy level also flow to the organization, management process, and information subsystem as corporate objectives, incentive compensation targets and leading and lagging indicators to be used to track performance.

Execution—Outcomes That Are, or Should Be, Knowable   Execution, also for purposes of this illustration, is depicted as a business unit activity conducted by a larger group of senior executives who have responsibility for the business units, major activities, and programs. Business unit planning follows the same logical path that was taken at the Strategy level looking forward one to three years. Those decisions are examined for their potential consequences and fit with the competencies and capabilities found within the value chain of the business unit.

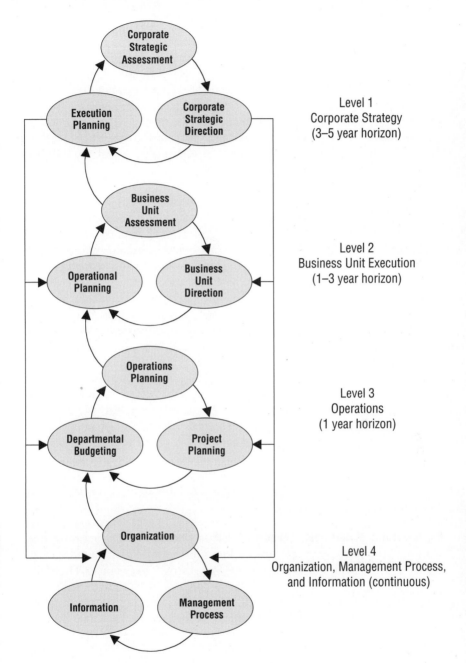

FIGURE 5.2 Levels of the Governance Model

Should there be an inconsistency between the outcomes at the execution level and those of the strategy level, the feedback loop to strategy triggers a reexamination of the strategic decisions until a balance is achieved. This interactive process is necessary to avoid any possible disconnect between strategy and execution. The decisions made at the execution level also flow to the operational level to enable operational planning to examine the operational consequences of decisions made at the execution level. Execution decisions also flow to the organization, management process, and information subsystem, again to monitor performance.

Operations—Outcomes Associated with the Present   The operations subsystem is defined as an activity/process or departmental planning and budgeting responsibility of operating management. The operational planning and budget responsibility is usually carried out by department and project managers looking forward for one year, and is a bottom-up process. Again, if for any reason the decisions made at the execution and strategy levels are found to be inconsistent with operational reality, those decisions must be recycled until there is a fit at all three levels. Operational and project metrics now form the one-year plans and budgets that feed into the organization, management process, and information subsystem.

Should there be an inconsistency between the outcomes at the execution level and those of the strategy level, the feedback loop to strategy triggers a reexamination of the strategic decisions until a balance is achieved. This interactive process is necessary to avoid any possible disconnect between strategy and execution. The decisions made at the execution level also flow to the operational level to enable operational planning to examine the operational consequences of decisions made at the execution level. Execution decisions also flow to the organization, management process, and information subsystem again to monitor performance.

Organization, Management Process, and Information   The organization, management process, and information subsystem, as indicated earlier, represents the tangible aspect of the System of Governance. The who, how, and what of decision making come together with the metrics necessary to plan and track performance. This subsystem receives information from all aspects of the Extended Enterprise and the environment and delivers that information, through management processes, to the board of directors, executive management, senior management, and operating management. The organization, management process, and information subsystem enables both the Governance Model and the System of Governance to function.

TOO MUCH PROCESS?

I am often confronted with the challenge, "All of this stuff is great in theory but won't work in practice." Of course, if it won't work in practice, the theory is no good. If process means three-ring binders full of policy, procedures, forms, checklists, and so on, the three-level decision-making model will drown in a sea of paperwork. The Governance Model and the System of Governance outlined in the next four chapters are a *framework*, not straitjacket. The framework is designed to bring people together with an agenda for decision making. The framework is intended to foster dialogue, learning, and feedback, not paperwork and compliance. The Governance Model and the System of Governance may be taught, practiced, and learned in any enterprise. The degree of formality and process, of course, depends on the complexity of the Extended Enterprise and the environment. Some decisions are famous for having been made on a napkin, such as the business model for Compaq Computer Corporation. Other decisions are of nearly infinite complexity, such as those faced by the oil companies during the 1970s. In any case, the frameworks must be tailored to the circumstances and implemented in a spirit of collegiality and teamwork. A hierarchical, top-down, command-and-control system of governance will yield the same fragmented, silo results that I described in Chapter 2.

When Do All of These Governance Model Activities Occur?

The Plan to Plan outlined in Chapter 10 (Figure 10.2) illustrates the calendar time frames that are followed on an annual basis. However, major decisions such as an acquisition or contemplated changes to strategy, execution, or operations decisions may call for the planning process to be opened up and the appropriate phases of the Governance Model used to plan the potential consequences of a particular transaction or decision. The Governance Model should be used as a framework for decision making regardless of when decisions need to be made.

DRILLING FURTHER DOWN INTO THE GOVERNANCE MODEL

This section provides examples drawn from actual client experiences at each level of the Governance Model. In each case, the choices and decisions are correlated directly with the potential or actual outcomes/ consequences in terms of rewards and risks associated with such choices and decisions. These examples have proved to be quite useful in communicating to boards and senior management the reality of the Governance Model.

Strategy—Outcomes Associated with the Future

The strategy subsystem, a positive (+) loop, deals with the variability of choices and decisions with the greatest degrees of uncertainty. Those choices and decisions deal with a future environment that we may only imagine. But imagine we must! The good news is that there are frameworks, methodologies, and tools available to assist us with our choices, decisions, and consequences.

Figure 5.3 provides examples of choices and decisions that characterize the strategy subsystem, together with the examples of the potential outcomes or consequences of those choices and decisions. It is always important to remember that outcomes or consequences at one level usually impact the choices and decisions available at all levels of the Extended Enterprise.

At the strategy level, the question or assertion is often made that the strategy was great but the execution was flawed. Probably there are situations where that assertion is true; however, from a Systems Thinking perspective, the potential unintended consequence of poor execution should have been contemplated. Generally, poor execution reflects a poor strategy

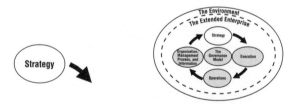

Choices and Decisions	Outcomes/Consequences, Rewards, and Risks
• Establish a framework and process for crisis management	• Timely and effective handling of "unexpected" events
• Establish a strategic direction which builds on competencies and capabilities to change the dynamics of the industry	• Creation of greater shareowner value based on growth of assets in place—"Beat the Fade"
• Establish a strategy which will influence public policy	• Less invasive regulation
• Implement a business model which will differentiate the firm	• Creation of greater shareowner value based on value-based pricing and customer retention
• Establish a leadership model and governance structure which recognizes the value of human resources	• Attract, develop, and retain high talent organization

FIGURE 5.3 Strategy—Outcomes Associated with the Future

because the reality or at least the uncertainty of an organization's capability to execute should have been a strategic issue. As I have heard Peter Drucker tell his students, "It is better to execute a poor strategy poorly than to execute a poor strategy well."

Execution—Outcomes That Are, or Should Be, Knowable

The execution subsystem, usually a negative (–) loop, deals with the competencies and capabilities that either are available within the Extended Enterprise or may be acquired within a relatively short time frame to execute strategy. Most implementation efforts either fail at this level or become so drawn out in time and space that whatever strategic advantage might have resulted is lost or at least watered down. Execution choices and decisions lead to outcomes and consequences that are largely knowable. If they aren't knowable, they should be.

Figure 5.4 provides examples of choices and decisions that characterize

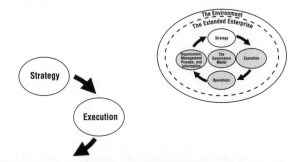

Choices and Decisions	Outcomes/Consequences, Rewards, and Risks
• Establish a culture which emphasizes the importance of effective program and project management, rigorous implementation, and accountability for results	• Speed to market—"first mover" advantages — Lower costs and greater leverage of high-talent resources
• Continuous improvement and tailoring of processes to leverage technology and improve customer relationships	• Improved margins through customer-value-added services
• Develop programs which examine the value of internal vs. external resources	• "Best Practices" of critical activities and processes lower unit costs
• Develop a system of management process and information	• Agenda for decision-making through shared information and knowledge
• Establish a "model" for merger/acquisition due diligence and implementation	• Achieve promised results of mergers and acquisitions

FIGURE 5.4 Execution—Outcomes That Are, or Should Be, Knowable

the execution subsystem; together with examples of the potential outcomes or consequences of those choices and decisions.

Execution is all about an organization's capability to change. Some organizations are really good at making changes with the result that their strategic decisions are quickly and effectively implemented and a competitive advantage is achieved—at least for a while. Through feedback and learning, an organization that is good at making changes can turn the execution loop from negative to positive. The ability to change becomes a strategic asset. The inability to change becomes a strategic liability.

Operations—Outcomes Associated with the Present

The operations subsystem—because it carries with it the reality that costs and revenue should be matched—is a negative feedback loop. That is good. The governance system must have a stabilizing influence or the enterprise will look like many of the dot-coms of the late 1990s.

The operations of many, if not most, organizations are on autopilot and run through sheer inertia. On balance, that is probably better than attempting to apply entrepreneurial energy to reinventing how each routine transaction should be processed. This is a level at which the word "bureaucracy" is not a bad word. Bureaucracies are supposed to provide efficient, predictable results. Operations activities should, however, provide feedback and learning to the strategy and execution subsystems in terms of what works and what does not work.

Figure 5.5 provides examples of choices and decisions together with the examples of potential outcomes and consequences of those choices and decisions.

Operations is "where the rubber meets the road," as they say. If the business model cannot be operated or won't work at the transaction level, then the business model and the strategy that "hatched" and executed the model also are wrong. If transaction risks occur that were not contemplated and which cannot be overcome, the operations subsystem is fatally flawed. Such flaws must be a part of the feedback and learning process.

Organization, Management Process, and Information

The final subsystem of the governance loop is a negative loop that brings the other subsystems together to assure that they are connected and are providing the organizational structure, management process, and information required to keep the governance system in balance. The organization, management process, and information subsystem provides the structure that every system requires in order to perform its function. From a Systems

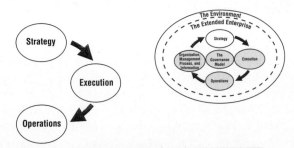

Choices and Decisions	Outcomes/Consequences, Rewards, and Risks
• Think beyond organizational "silos" or parochial boundaries	• Lower risk profile for entire enterprise
• Develop templates or methodologies which provide for continuous monitoring of known risks and which provide for organizational learning around unintended consequences	• Lower risk profile and greater organizational learning
• Continuously monitor opportunities for transferring risk through capital markets and insurance	• Lower cost and less volatility
• Rigorously enforce regulatory compliance and seek competitive advantage	• Culture of ethics and integrity across the enterprise

FIGURE 5.5 Operations—Outcomes Associated with the Present

Thinking perspective, organization, management process, and information comprise the intangible catalyst that enables the entire system to work. All systems in nature and successful commerce require some form of structure, which is never visible. The organization, management process, and information subsystem becomes visible and tangible and serves as a catalyst by means of:

- Organization of the enterprise—who does what.
- Management process—how the organization works.
- Information—the leading and lagging indicators that portray feedback and learning and form the basis for board and management action.

The organization, management process, and information subsystem is an integral element not only of the Governance Model but of the Extended Enterprise as a complete system. Just as was stated earlier in this chapter, if the Governance Model is the system, organization, management process, and information provide the organizing force that enables the system to function. The subsystem is not an appendage or something bolted on to something else. It is not some form of memo or special purpose system. The organization, management process, and information subsystem is the instrument panel of the Extended Enterprise.

BIG DECISIONS

Each of the following chapters has a section called "Big Decisions." Based on my consulting, teaching, research, and general observations of effective and ineffective decision making, I have categorized what I believe to be the Big Decisions to be considered at each level of the Governance Model. There is plenty of leeway within any enterprise to question, add, or delete what I classify as Big Decisions. My choices of decisions, however, should be considered as at least a starting point for consideration.

Strategy
- Crisis management
- Nature of the enterprise
- Actions of competitors and regulators
- Allocation of resources

Execution
- Market segmentation
- Value chain

Operations
- Communications/dialogue
- Attention to detail

Organization, Management Process, and Information
- One information system
- Keep it simple
- Precision is not required
- Fast-track implementation

As you read these chapters, think about the Big Decisions that characterize your organization. Remember, a decision not to do something may have equal or greater consequences than a decision to do something.

MANAGEMENT

Each of the following four chapters also has a section that outlines the activities I term as management:

- Roles of those having the greatest decision-making accountability and responsibility.
- Processes/activities that are often found within a particular subsystem.

■ Methodologies available, including tools and techniques used to facilitate decision making.

Taken together across the Extended Enterprise, Big Decisions and Management represent starting points for organizations to implement a Governance Model and a System of Governance. The important take-away point is this: All of the separate management activities found within the enterprise should come together to form systems. Systems Thinking is all about bringing those subsystems together which are truly required for the system to function as a whole and discarding those activities which do not contribute to the whole—the pieces of twine. Think about the Governance Model as the toolbox and the roles and responsibilities, processes, and activities, and methodologies as the tools contained within that box. Over time, the tools may change, but the box remains the same.

CONCLUSION

Now you have the whole picture. You can not only see the entire system of governance and risk, but you also have gotten a glimpse of the subsystems that comprise the whole. This system perspective is nonlinear; it deals with cause and effect, but with the added dimension of time and space, and provides for feedback and learning. The system is grounded in science and views the world and its interconnectedness as reality. The following chapters examine each of the subsystems that comprise the whole and without which there would be no whole.

CHAPTER 6

Strategy—Outcomes Associated with the Future

INTRODUCTION

All of our choices and decisions deal with degrees of uncertainty around the outcomes of those choices and decisions—risks and rewards. By its very nature, strategy is about the future, a future that is not only unknown, but perhaps unknowable. Should we give up and leave the future to chance rather than choice? Of course not! There is a great deal that we can do to increase the number of choices available to us and to improve the quality of the outcomes of the decisions that result from those choices. This chapter is all about the frameworks, processes, and methodologies available, not to predict the future, but rather to anticipate and gain a better understanding of that future. This chapter will also extend the idea of the System of Governance to the roles of the board and executive management in strategic decision making.

BIG DECISIONS

Systems Thinking and the implications of cause and effect and feedback and learning define the strategy subsystem and the major choices and decisions that comprise strategy:

- Crisis management.
- Nature of the enterprise.
- Actions of competitors and regulators.
- Allocation of resources.

There is probably an infinite number of choices and decisions that deal with the future. The four areas outlined should have sufficient scope to deal with most choices and related decisions boards and executive management face. Each of the subsystems will discuss the nature of the decisions available to the board and executive management.

The strategic choices and decisions available to the board and executive management are only the starting point for thinking about the outcomes—consequences—of those choices and decisions. The strategy loop of the governance model feeds the execution loop, the operations loop, and the organization, management process, and information loop. Those loops, in turn, provide feedback and learning to the strategy loop.

Crisis Management

We have defined strategies as those choices and decisions we make, or don't make, about the future—choices and decisions whose outcomes are largely unknown and often unknowable. How is it then that we include crisis management in the category of decision making called strategy?

In many ways, we think about risk and reward (or problems and opportunities) in terms of chance—good or bad luck. Events occur over which we have no forewarning, much less control. Crises, which are the outcomes or results of some event, may take many forms, and by definition provide no forewarning. However, we have considerable control over the choices and decisions we make around how we handle such crises. We may therefore do as much as is humanly possible to mitigate or enhance the consequences of such crises. We can't manage the crises' outcomes directly, but we can manage what we do from the board of directors onward throughout the Extended Enterprise to assure that outcomes are as favorable as they can be.

From a governance perspective, we know that both good and bad things happen without warning. It is the role of the board and executive management to anticipate how crises may occur and to assure that processes are in place that help to define what we do when the unexpected actually happens. This is the essence of crisis management.[1]

Some Examples   The feedback and learning that took place following the 1993 bombing of the World Trade Center is credited with saving thousands of lives on 9/11. The crises brought about by terrorists' acts may occur unexpectedly, but there is no reason in today's world for such events to be unanticipated.

The Johnson & Johnson Tylenol crisis could have brought down the company. Its brands might have been forever destroyed. Those outcomes did not occur because the board and management anticipated and took action around such an eventuality as a result of having in place the culture (the J&J Creed) and processes for dealing with the unexpected. Johnson & Johnson took responsibility for the situation and did something immediately. The J&J brands have never been stronger.

By contrast, TWA was ultimately brought down by the Flight 800 disaster. The board and management reacted late and without much substance, thereby destroying the trust and integrity that had been in place since the founding of the company. TWA did not take responsibility and did little for a very long time following the crash.

There are numerous examples of disasters and the crises brought about as a result of those disasters—some of which actually enhanced the value of the enterprise and some of which destroyed the enterprise. The Governance Model must first anticipate the nature of disasters that may produce crises for the enterprise, understand the consequences of such crises, and then take action to develop the processes that may be invoked when such unexpected events occur.

The words *anticipate*, *understand*, and *take action* appear often in this book. Hopefully, using these words in the specific context of a disaster that, in turn, produces various crises will provide helpful illustrations of the power of those words.

There has been a great deal written about crisis management and disaster recovery planning. The critical issue here is to assure that whatever processes are put in place are considered as a part of the Governance Model and the System of Governance. Crisis management at the board and executive management levels is just as much a part of the enterprise loop as the operational and technical details of disaster planning and recovery are at the operations level. For example, the ability of the New York securities firms, the stock exchanges, and the communications networks to get up and running quickly following 9/11 is attributed to the effective planning that took place following the terrorist attack on the World Trade Center in 1993 and preparations for Y2K.

Nature of the Enterprise

The primary role of the board and executive management, as we pointed out earlier, is the survival of the firm and the creation of value for the share owners. The survival of the firm deals with all of the so-called stakeholders of the Extended Enterprise, including:

- Employees
- Customers
- Providers/suppliers/partners

■ Regulators
■ Communities

The creation of value for the share owners, of course, deals with the owners—the suppliers of capital. The board and executive management walk a fine line in balancing the interests of all of the stakeholders with those of the owners. No strategic decision calls attention to those self-interests as do the decisions around the nature of the enterprise.

Continuously refining the nature of the enterprise is a prerequisite to both survival and the creation of shareholder value. Organizations are either growing or dying. While there may be an apparent status quo maintained for years, the reality is that to survive the business must be in a constant state of innovation and renewal around the nature of the enterprise itself.

What Do We Mean by Nature of the Enterprise?   Peter Drucker has a unique set of three questions, which, while appearing to be simple, obvious, and straightforward, frame the issues of the nature of the enterprise in a very useful way:

1. What is our business?
2. Who are our customers?
3. What do our customers value?

The first question Peter is asking is about the theory of the firm or, in today's vernacular, the business model. What business are we in? We know many enterprises that either answer that question in the past tense or can't answer the question at all. Yet, in terms of governance and risk, the choices available and the decisions made by the board and executive management have a significant impact on survival and the creation of value. Nondecisions or decisions to do nothing have an equally profound effect. An obsolete business model or maintenance of the status quo until the model no longer works may be the disservice that a director may perform in his or her governance role.

For example, Kmart, the former S. S. Kresge Company, shed its five-and-dime mentality in the 1960s, reinvented itself as a high-level discount department store, and survived, while W. T. Grant, S. J. Korvette, and F. W. Woolworth literally died. But Kmart failed to learn from its own and others' successes. It took another 30 years, but Kmart filed for bankruptcy in 2002, while Wal-Mart and Target survived and grew. Where were Kmart's directors during the 1970s and 1980s when the business model became obsolete? What happened to corporate governance?

Xerox is another example of an obsolete business model and an absence of an effective System of Governance. Over the past 50 years Xerox pioneered and originated a great number of innovations in computer technology. Xerox failed to integrate any of its innovative developments—from the mouse to icons to an early lead in scientific computing to its own core product—the copier. What happened? Xerox was in the high-end copying business and no other. Each new niche brought about by technology—technology pioneered by Xerox—went to competitors. Where were the directors during the decades when Xerox fell from grace?

Alternately, consider Intel, the Silicon Valley chipmaker. Intel, with its board and its management soundly grounded in science and technology, has reinvented its industry and its company every 18 months for the past 25 years. It had to, or it would have followed into oblivion the majority of the enterprises spawned in Silicon Valley over the past generation. Intel may not have characterized its performance as a shining example of great governance, but it was, and continues to be an excellent example of best practices not only in governance but in culture and values as well.

The WellPoint Story   Our list of winners and losers in corporate governance could go on and on. However, one further example of the metamorphosis of an enterprise through the difficult transformation of its business model will illustrate both issues of survival and the creation of shareholder value. The transformation of WellPoint, introduced in Chapter 1, from a nearly defunct, not-for-profit Blue Cross of California in 1985 into the managed health care leader of today, and the creation of a $4 billion endowment for the betterment of the people of California is an important story of board and executive management governance.

WellPoint Health Networks Inc. rose like phoenix from the ashes of a badly executed merger of two not-for-profit Blue Cross plans. A new CEO, Leonard Schaeffer, was hired to turn the combination around after failures of culture and values, systems and operations, and basic competency of management. Blue Cross of California, from which WellPoint was to spring, was faced with many choices and decisions—from its business model to its organization to the development of an organizational capability to execute on its strategies. WellPoint considered numerous choices around the form of its business model from its then combination of geography and function to either geography or function or to a possible business unit structure. The alternatives, including the consequences of each, were played out, particularly from the standpoint of meeting the differing needs of the various markets served by the company. Other issues such as the availability of general managers who could actually run a business were considered. The risks associated with either a functional or a geographic structure or some combination of the two were thought through in terms of much needed accountability and responsibility for execution. The question of alignment of the activities in the value chain was considered in order to directly match cost and revenue and hence profitability. The potential outcomes of the available choices were considered as the risks associated with the decision. For example, Leonard and the board felt that simply putting new people in old positions brought about the huge risk that the inertia and status quo of the old structure could not be changed in time to turn the company around, if ever.

Finally, the decision was made to create three vertically integrated units called market business units (MBUs). The three units, each faced off against a specific market segment, would be managed by general managers who had to be recruited from outside the company. The general managers would be responsible for all of the revenue from their markets as well as the costs and resulting profitability (or loss) from specific sets of customers. The "ownership" of a business and the sense of accountability and responsibility for serving customers profitably changed the culture and capabilities of management at all levels to operate their business in ways that simply would not have been possible with other choices of structure.

From 1985 to 1993, Blue Cross of California turned around from being the least successful "Blue" plan to become one of the most successful while serving the most competitive markets in the country. In 1993, a for-profit corporation, WellPoint Health Networks, was formed and taken public as the owner and operator of Blue Cross of California's commercial business. Subsequently, Blue Cross of California completed a lengthy regulatory review process, converted to for-profit status, and made what was ultimately a $4 billion contribution to charity. WellPoint along with its major subsidiary Blue Cross went on to become one of the most successful managed health care companies in the nation.

Let's go back and examine the original decision to form the three MBUs. The choices available were all about the nature of the enterprise or the business model. The potential outcomes of the decision—the risks and rewards—included:

■ Looking like every other "Blue" plan and maybe crawling from last to the middle of the pack.

■ Doing nothing and hoping that the external environment would "float all boats on the same tide."

The safest decision, when considered at the time, was to look like every other "Blue" plan. After all, who would criticize a decision to look like scores of other companies in the same industry?

The decision to form MBUs, while appearing to be the riskiest, was considered by Leonard and the board to be the safest in terms of both intended and unintended consequences. Knowing which market segments were the most and least profitable would enable management to exit the unprofitable business quickly. In a turnaround situation, no other decision provided that outcome. Developing managers who understood their customers and how to serve them profitably not only greatly accelerated the turnaround but actually achieved extraordinary profitability in what was considered to be the "dog" market—the consumer business. A young leader, Mark Weinberg, was recruited to run that business and immediately saw the opportunity to serve the consumer market in ways heretofore not considered possible. Mark made execution decisions and created an operational capability that is today the model for many of WellPoint's competitors.

Another leader, Ron Williams, now president of Aetna, was recruited to run the so-called group or corporate MBU. By now in Blue Cross' evolution, it was clear that serving large corporate customers was, at best, marginally profitable. Ron, a superb operations executive, fine-tuned his MBU to the point that growth and profitability were achieved in an extremely competitive national market for large group customers.

Coming back to choices and decisions, Leonard Schaeffer and the board made a decision about the nature of the enterprise that saved the company and formed the basis for the 17-year run of growth and profitability. Our board and executive management governance tests of survival and creation of value for share owners were clearly met. Changing the nature of the enterprise achieved both outcomes.

Actions of Competitors and Regulators

The environment loop introduced the complexity affecting choices and decisions brought about by competition. Every enterprise, of course, faces competition in one form or another. How the board and executive management deal with the choices available often makes the difference in results or outcomes—risks and rewards—of the entire enterprise. From a strategy perspective, the real competition most often comes from the most unexpected quarters. It is the responsibility of the board and executive management, as a part of the System of Governance, to anticipate and understand the implications of competitor action before such action changes the environment in which the enterprise operates.

For example, it is not clear to me that any of the major retailers saw the coming of Wal-Mart or Home Depot. Perhaps it was not possible for either the large general retailers or the specialty chains to anticipate the impact that those two fast-moving emerging competitors would have on their business or industry. I see the phenomenon of the retailers missing emerging competitors much the same way that Detroit missed the Japanese automakers during the 1960s.

What Should the Board Be Doing?　　What choices are available to the boards and executive management when situations such as the impact of Wal-Mart and Home Depot on the external environment happen? How should the System of Governance have worked? First, any board or executive management group that is not continuously tracking new entrants is not doing its job. Anticipating and understanding the potential consequences of new entrants or unexpected moves of existing competitors is an ongoing process of assessing cause and effect, feedback and learning from the environment loop. The board in its role as the driver of the System of Governance is doing its job only if it is pushing the discussion around the potential consequences of the actions of existing and potential competitors.

Members of the board, if they are to be truly effective, must understand at a detail level the external environment in which the Extended Enterprise operates. Each of the subsystems of the environment loop, including social forces, public policy, and competition and capital markets, may become agenda items for board meetings. In particular, actions of competitors signal emerging changes in the environment that the board must anticipate and understand. The emergence of niche players may foretell a market segment not being properly served. Merger activity may signal that a competitor is acquiring competencies not previously available. Sudden changes in profit margins may indicate significant differences in cost structures or, as recent events suggest, improper accounting. The familiarity of the individual board members with specific competitors will go a long way toward mitigating the impact of unexpected action on the part of competitors and enable the board to fulfill their role in the System of Governance. More than that, the board will not utter the now familiar refrain, "No one ever told us."

Allocation of Resources

The Governance Model, in particular the strategy loop and the System of Governance, have as a principal focus the allocation of resources. Indeed, strategy is really implemented through resource allocation decisions. Such decisions establish the outcomes that either mitigate the degree of risk an organization truly undertakes or maximize the opportunities available from investment decisions. In any case, the board and executive management exercise their governance responsibilities by means of their resource allocation decisions.

Before getting into the nature of the resources to be allocated, let's consider for a moment a tangible example of an absence of feedback and learning around the capital investment decisions of most enterprises. In a static (versus dynamic) world of many decision-making processes, capital investment decisions are meticulously analyzed by the board and executive management, refined and approved, and incorporated into the capital expense budget for the coming year. And that is the end of it! The amount of feedback that would compare actual to target returns is virtually nonexistent in most enterprises. Resource allocation decisions are Big Decisions; however, an understanding of the outcomes of those decisions is generally absent.

What Resources? The following organizational resources, while presented at a high level, depict the areas within the enterprise loop that are critical to the strategic direction of the enterprise, its survival, and growth.

- Human capital.
- Customer relationships/long-term value.
- Long-term contracts.
- Financial capital.
- Knowledge and information.
- Physical facilities and processes.
- Technology.
- Brands, trademarks, patents, and valuable formulas.

The choices and decisions around the allocation of these resources within the enterprise will largely define the outcomes—risks and rewards—of the enterprise.

In other words, how people are developed, retained, and allocated to the most promising opportunities determines the success of a particular strategic initiative. How customer relationships are developed, maintained, and valued over the long term creates the purpose of the enterprise.

Most of the categories of resources listed do not appear on the balance sheet and are not accounted for in traditional ways. Yet the allocation of these resources to the most promising opportunities makes a greater difference to the sustainability and profitable growth than the investment dollars being acquired through debt and equity offerings or retained earnings and allocated through traditional capital allocation decisions.

Some Examples   Human capital is the primary resource of Nordstrom. Human capital, while not appearing on the Nordstrom balance sheet, drives the strategy of the company. When Nordstrom opened up the Southern California market in the late 1980s, the decision to name Betsy Sanders as the leader represented an allocation of a resource that established the successful outcome of the strategy. Betsy, who had managed the human resource activities of the company at a corporate level, was the ideal executive to build the team to compete in Southern California. Indeed, Betsy's leadership created a $1 billion business in Southern California.[2]

Customer relationships/long-term value do not appear on the balance sheet of Edward Jones, the investment and brokerage firm based in St. Louis. Led by John Bachmann, another Drucker protégé, the firm—still a partnership—has more offices and long-term customers than any of its famous Wall Street counterparts. When Peter Drucker teaches us, "The purpose of the corporation is to create a customer," Edward Jones takes Peter literally. The customer resource and the long-term value created by that resource comprise the primary resource allocation strategy of the enterprise. Opening new offices around the world, hiring brokers to serve those customers, and keeping those customers by not pushing in-house products or investment advice have created a customer-centric powerhouse. The examination of the choices available and the decisions made from among those choices created outcomes far different from any of Edward Jones' competitors. The feedback and learning from the customers and brokers not only created the Governance Model, but also made the System of Governance the way of doing business.

It should be clear from the foregoing examples of successful Governance Models and Systems of Governance that choices available and the decisions made from among those choices led to the successful outcomes of WellPoint, Intel, Nordstrom, and Edward Jones. All four of these organizations may be characterized as having strong, proactive boards and solid leaders.

Those boards and those leaders, often by intuition, but mostly by a collegial attitude of dialogue, feedback, and learning, have built sustainable, successful businesses. They selected business models, watched the actions of their competitors, and allocated resources in ways that created strategic directions that were uniquely successful. This is what governance is all about. That is the role of effective boards and executive management.

MANAGEMENT

As I pointed out in Chapter 5, I am using the term "management" to illustrate:

- Roles of those having the greatest decision-making accountability and responsibility.
- Processes/activities that are often found within a particular subsystem.
- Methodologies available, including tools and techniques used to facilitate decision making.

Roles and Responsibilities

The strategy subsystem of the Governance Model is really the domain of the board and executive management. Gone are the days when the CEO and his or her team would make a presentation to the board regarding the future of the enterprise and adjourn for lunch. The System of Governance begins with the board as a strategic partner with the CEO. Through an open, questioning dialogue between the board and executive management, strategy just gets better. The board, assuming that the members understand the enterprise model and its relationship to the environment model, is in a unique position, not to second-guess the CEO or to develop strategy independent of the CEO, but to collaborate with the CEO to make the best decisions from the choices available.

The board and executive management also have the responsibility to anticipate, understand, and take action around the consequences, intended and unintended, of the strategic decisions that are made. Asking questions around the execution and operational outcomes triggered or potentially triggered by the strategic action is the job of the board and senior management. The board and executive management must also assure themselves that the management process and information subsystem of the Governance Model is providing the feedback necessary to track the outcomes of the decisions made and to assure that learning is taking place.

Finally, I have worked with a lot of companies that get into trouble as a result of what might be called unintended consequences. Most of the time when I interview board members after the fact, I hear the familiar refrain, "No one told us." By now, my response invariably is, "Why didn't you ask?" The future survival and growth of the enterprise is the job of the board and executive management. There is no excuse for their not performing their jobs.

Processes/Activities

Outcomes associated with the future, as we have indicated many times in this chapter, are all about dealing with uncertainty. The board and executive management have a wide range of processes and activities available to help anticipate, understand, and take action in the environment of uncertainty.

The first issue of process within the strategy subsystem of the Governance Model is the level of the enterprise for which strategy is being developed. For the purpose of this discussion, the level is that of the corporation. The next chapter, which deals with execution, will discuss planning at the business unit level. From the perspective of the corporation, strategy deals with the issues of survival and value creation for share owners. Taken in that light, corporate strategy should deal with how the corporation creates value. When we consider corporate governance, the two issues that drive corporate value address the role of the corporation versus the roles of its businesses.

If the role of the corporation is that of a portfolio manager, the corporation creates relatively little value that investors could not create on their own. As outlined earlier in this chapter, it is my belief that long-term survival and value creation dictate that the corporation itself create value through the determination of:

- The nature of the enterprise.
- An understanding of the actions of competitors.
- Allocation of resources.

Boards and executive management that either leave these choices and decisions to business units or are not actively and intellectually engaged in the process are simply not doing their jobs.

The Strategy Loop   The strategic processes and activities that create value for the corporation and that outline what the board and executive management should be doing also form a loop of cause and effect, feedback and learning. The strategy loop (shown in Figure 6.1) may be designed to look forward for as many as five years for most industries.

The strategic assessment phase deals with the question, "*What* will it take to win?" That is, given the nature of the factors of the external environment together with the value creation activities of the Extended Enterprise, what does the organization have to do to achieve a sustainable competitive advantage—that is, to survive and grow?

The strategic direction phase deals with the question, "*How* will we win?" Specifically, what corporate strategies will be required to sustain and grow the corporation? The linkage between the strategic assessment and strategic direction is direct; the two relate to each other in a cause-and-effect manner. Feedback and learning take place when the strategies are tested against the findings of the strategic assessment phase.

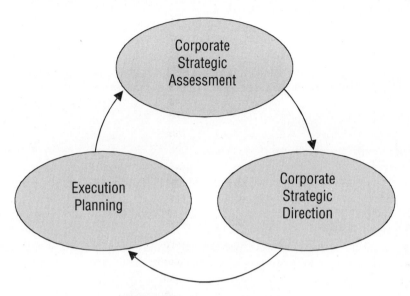

FIGURE 6.1 The Strategy Loop

The execution planning phase is intended to answer the question, "*Who* will be responsible?" At this point in the strategy loop, issues that will affect execution are addressed. The work of execution planning provides insight into exactly who will carry the strategies forward and be responsible for their execution. Feedback and learning between the execution planning phase and strategic assessment and strategic direction test the feasibility of the strategies developed.

Methodologies Available

There is a wide range of methodologies available to assist the board and executive management to assess the choices available and to help to anticipate, understand, and take action around the decisions they may make. Some methodologies are intended to assist in anticipating the uncertainties around future outcomes and are quite subjective in their approach. Other methodologies are more quantitative in their approach. To me the first principle associated with the selection of a methodology is the reality that multiple tools will be required to do the job. For example, I have experienced one school of thought that asserts that real option theory, which is briefly discussed later in this chapter, is the one and only, all-purpose tool that is required for decision making. Beware of any single school of thought. The world is not that simple.

We will briefly discuss each of the following methodologies, which, used in combination with one another, help the board and executive management deal with the uncertainties associated with the future:

- Scenario planning
- Game theory
- Mathematical modeling

There are countless variations on these methodologies, some designed with a focus on a particular industry.

Scenario Planning   An important tool in the forward-looking process of examining the external environment is the technique known as scenario planning.[3] Pioneered by Peter Schwartz, then at Shell Oil, the technique helps to anticipate the future through the creation of stories or scenarios. Such scenarios take current assumptions around demographics and other drivers of the future and create logical, internally consistent stories around what the future may be for a particular industry or Extended Enterprise.

It is not the intention of scenario planning to forecast or predict the future. Probabilities are not used. What is helpful is the idea that the future could take three or four very logical forms. In reality, the future does not take any of the forms played out. However, from a board and executive management standpoint, the value is found in reaching agreement around the relatively few actions that the enterprise might undertake *regardless* of which view of the future begins to take shape. The strategic objective of survival and sustainability is achieved regardless of what happens.

Scenario planning is a technique often used in connection with annual board and executive management planning sessions. During the course of the strategic assessment phase outlined in the preceding "Processes/Activities" section, the board and executive management come together with the staff work already completed in terms of alternative scenarios, and engage in dialogue around the consequences of the various stories for the enterprise. A good facilitator will draw out the common themes from among the scenarios and work with the participants to establish the conclusions that will be effective regardless of what the future holds.

The strategic conclusions arrived at as a result of the scenario planning exercise are integrated with other analyses which are described later to arrive at a comprehensive and shared view of the future uncertainties and what we may do to survive and grow in view of those uncertainties.

Game Theory   Early in this chapter, we established the actions of competitors as a key consideration to the anticipation and understanding of the consequences of choices and decisions associated with the strategy subsystem of the Governance Model. Game theory is a methodology pioneered by the military and CIA in an attempt to anticipate potential enemy actions under a wide range of assumptions. Using probability theory and Monte Carlo simulation techniques, software is available to process the millions of potential outcomes and establish most likely or probable outcomes. Game theory is another tool available to boards and executive management to help think through the various what-if consequences of the actions of Competitors. The idea is, once again, to open up the dialogue among the participants and to assist them to engage in deep conversations about the future and the consequences of our actions. Game theory, when combined with scenario planning, provides a powerful quantitative, left-brain exercise to complement the more qualitative, right-brain work of scenario planning.

Mathematical Modeling   For the "quant," there are always the very sophisticated, presumably objective mathematical tools that help one to understand and make choices from among a variety of options and alternative investments for the purposes of the allocation of resources. Among the most common tools are the familiar discounted cash flow (DCF) and net present value (NPV). Among the more recent additions to the tool kit are real options theory and economic modeling. Like most tools, these are useful for specific purposes and should be used with an understanding of both their limitations and the reality that multiple tools are usually required to complete any task.

For many years, DCF and NPV techniques were the most favored tools for analyzing the uncertainties and timing of long-term investments. These are useful, simple tools, particularly for analyzing alternative capital investments among a portfolio of potential uses of capital.

Real option[4] theory, alluded to earlier, is thought by some to be the "universal tool." I am always very careful with the use of so-called universal tools. Real option theory does more closely reflect the manner in which management really makes financial bets about the future. Real option theory and the mathematical models made practical with today's computing power enable the board and executive management to treat resource allocation decisions with the same logic as that of call options on a stock.

The strength of the real option theory, as with call options, is the ability to be flexible in the face of uncertainty. For example, if the economic value of the proposed investment decision is thought of as the face value of the stock, the degree of uncertainty around the value of that investment or stock determines whether or not to proceed with the investment. The mathematics of real option models enable the decision maker to trigger the option under different timing circumstances that depict the value of the option or decision to invest. Uncertainty is the driver of timing decisions when using real option theory. As we have discussed throughout this section, the outcomes of our decisions are unknown and often unknowable depending on the time horizon and the uncertainty of the outcome. Real option theory provides the tools to enable an organization to better understand when to exercise the option.

Economic modeling is another tool for the board and executive management to help develop and test future outcomes using what-if assumptions. Most economic models, because they are so industry and enterprise specific, are "home grown" and are developed over time as the members of the board and executive management gain learning from their use. Economic models of the enterprise may be used to test the various assumptions that drive growth and profitability and serve as useful tools for quickly recycling those outcomes. Economic models further assist in understanding the sensitivity of the various assumptions on the anticipated outcome.

I hope that this brief overview of what I call management is helpful in the sense that there are tools available that help one to anticipate and understand the future consequences of choices and decisions. I hope that I have also made the point that no single tool is the only right tool, and that all tools are only as good as the craftsmen who use them. As a partner of mine once asserted, "A fool with a tool is still a fool."

CONCLUSION

As we stated at the beginning of the strategy subsystem of the Governance Model, we are dealing with outcomes associated with the future, outcomes that are largely unknown and often unknowable. The Governance Model is intended to provide the board and executive management with a framework for considering the future, from crisis management to the allocation of resources, as well as the identification of some widely accepted tools to help them to do their job. More importantly, the System of Governance highlights the roles and responsibilities of the board and executive management in terms of how they do their job. The System of Governance is not about legal and regulatory compliance, sign-off, and checklists; it is about *how* the Extended Enterprise anticipates, understands, and takes action around the consequences of its choices and decisions. It is vital that the board and executive management get it right as they make big bets about an uncertain future.

NOTES

1. Steven Link, *Crisis Management, Planning for the Inevitable* (New York: American Management Association/AMACOM, 1986).
2. Betsy Sanders and Bonnie Jameson, *Fabled Service: Ordinary Acts, Extraordinary Outcomes* (San Francisco: Jossey-Bass, 1997).
3. Peter Schwartz, *The Art of the Long View* (New York: Doubleday, 1991).
4. Avinash K. Dixit and Robert S. Pindyck, "The Options Approach to Capital Investment," *Harvard Business Review* (May–June 1995): 106.

Execution—Outcomes That Are, or Should Be, Knowable

INTRODUCTION

Execution is the "transmission" or "gearbox" that links the "engine" of strategy with the "wheels" of operations. As stated earlier, a poor strategy well executed is a losing strategy; a great strategy poorly executed is also a losing strategy. The metaphor of a vehicle transmission is useful in that it is the transmission that buffers the speed of the engine and coordinates it with the speed of the wheels to provide smooth tracking of the wheels with the road. Obviously, if the engine was directly connected to the wheels, the wheels would be uncontrollable or even come off. If the connection was too loose, the engine would spin uselessly and the wheels would not gain any traction. As explained in the preceding chapter, the purpose of strategy is to achieve a fit of the Extended Enterprise with the environment. The purpose of execution is to provide a fit between strategy and the operations of the Extended Enterprise.

This chapter is intended to build the linkage between the execution planning subsystem of the strategy loop and the choices and decisions required for successful implementation of that strategy. This chapter also builds on the strategic planning process described in the previous chapter to create a business planning process that develops strategy at the business unit level. Finally, in order for the outcomes of execution to be knowable, the choices and decisions initiated during the development of strategy must be anticipated, understood, and acted upon during the execution of that strategy. The first principle of Systems Thinking is, once again, consideration of the whole before the parts.

BIG DECISIONS

Systems Thinking and the implications of cause and effect and feedback and learning define the execution subsystem and the major choices and decisions that comprise execution:

■ Market segmentation
■ Value chain

These decisions are a continuation of our efforts to answer the three Peter Drucker questions raised in the previous chapter:

1. What is our business?
2. Who are our customers?
3. What do our customers value?

Other decisions will undoubtedly be discovered during the business planning process—decisions that will be unique to the enterprise or the industry.

In particular, the focus of the execution loop is the answer to detailed questions about the needs, wants, and expectations of our customers as well as the means of creating value for those customers. The following sections will provide the specifics around the choices and decisions to be made by senior management during the business planning process.

Market Segmentation

Peter Drucker's first question—"What is our business?"—forces the question of served markets to be answered in strategic terms. Broad choices around demographics, psychographics, and geographics are answered when the business model is created in the strategy loop. For example, the WellPoint business model contemplated three served markets—consumers, corporations, and government—and business units were established to serve those markets.

The next question—"Who are our customers?"—is a much deeper question. The choices available and the decisions made at the execution level become very specific around target markets.

Some Examples   From a governance and risk perspective, it is interesting to examine how and by whom the decision was made by several large insurance companies to offer homeowners insurance to owners of mobile homes in the Hurricane Alley of South Florida. No one could have known on a definitive basis that another "storm of the century," Hurricane Andrew, would wipe out most of the mobile homes in the area. However, the weather patterns in South Florida and the vulnerability of mobile homes are known by insurance executives. The outcome, therefore, of the decision to serve the South Florida market segment of mobile home owners with property and casualty insurance was "knowable." It was not a question of "if," but of "when."

Shorebank Corporation in Chicago has done a wonderful job for over 30 years in the "underserved" market of the Hyde Park section of the South Side of Chicago. Under the leadership of Ronald Grzywinski, chairman, and Mary Houghton, president, Shorebank has understood the market very well and been able to meet the needs, wants, and expectations of low-income, minority customers with great success. Shorebank is able to service and create shareholder value in neighborhoods where the so-called big banks have not been able to compete. Shorebank's choices and decisions have produced outcomes without the risks perceived by the larger banks. In other words, because Shorebank knows its market and target customers, the bank can offer uniquely tailored services, whereas the big banks can offer only their generic, off-the-shelf products. The difference has created considerable value at lower risk for the bank. Shorebank has further enhanced its market position with a unique combination of community development efforts, a strategy not available to its traditional competitors. Having a social conscience as well as an economic incentive provides great value to all stakeholders.

For a generation, Citicorp, now Citigroup, has been a powerhouse consumer bank. The choices and decisions made by Walter Wriston and John Reed in the 1970s led to a capability to profitably serve various consumer market segments in New York—segments that the other big New York banks decided not to serve with the same intensity. Not only did the bank survive and grow throughout the next 20 years, it did so without having to merge with other New York banks. Citicorp benefited from the feedback and learning from its success in New York to go on to establish profitable consumer franchises in nearly every corner of the world. Citicorp's strategy called for business units that matched its customers. Citicorp's execution provided the capabilities and competencies not only to segment the consumer market but to deliver services that customers needed, wanted, and expected. Citicorp's choices and decisions produced outcomes that forced the actions of its competitors as well as changes to the regulatory landscape.

Where Is the Risk?   The work of segmenting markets is well documented and understood throughout the services and consumer products industries. The execution of strategy based on carefully selected segmentation efforts is another story. Said another way, most organizations claim to be customer-focused, to listen to their customers, and to respond to the needs of their customers. The reality is that most enterprises, when it comes to execution of such strategy, are still quite inwardly focused. The decisions necessary to focus on the customer are generally not made. The execution of a market segment–focused strategy is a governance and risk issue that belongs to senior management. The choices and decisions of senior management to organize the value creation activities around the customer, in order to focus on that customer, are neither anticipated nor understood, much less acted upon.

The risks associated with not being focused on the customer run the gamut from trying to be all things to all people to permitting new competitors to cherry pick the most profitable segments. In many ways, actions of competitors are brought about by inaction of so-called entrenched market leaders.

Another WellPoint Example   The WellPoint customer-focused business model was described in some depth in the previous chapter. WellPoint executed on that business model with such effectiveness that 17 years later their competitors still "don't get it." If WellPoint had not executed superbly at that time, and continuously ever since, the enterprise would have neither survived nor provided the value that were the ultimate outcomes of the well-executed strategy.

WellPoint first reduced the strategic and execution risks associated with its business model by very careful market segmentation. The execution of the strategy was not designed to reduce insurance risk, because the pooling of large populations holds costs and prices down for all members of the population. Rather the strategy and execution were designed to understand exactly what the customer needed and then implement an efficient delivery system to meet those needs.

Leonard Schaeffer, Mark Weinberg, and Ron Williams carefully designed their organizations not only to be focused on the specifics of the segments within the business units, but also to align all of the activities in the value chain to meet those customer needs. Activities that did not add value for a particular segment were eliminated along with their costs. These were execution decisions, the outcomes of which have served the stakeholders and stockholders very well.

Focus on the Customer   Market segmentation activities are made up of choices and decisions, the execution of which produces knowable outcomes—risks and rewards. The operative word in market segmentation is *focus*. The focus of the business units must be on the customer—today, tomorrow, and forever. Today's needs change. They must be anticipated, understood, and acted upon as they change. Decisions by senior management must not only produce profitable growth in the short term; they must assure that by anticipating and meeting future needs they lock out emerging competitors in advance. Market segmentation choices and decisions further reinforce the Drucker perspective, "The purpose of the enterprise is to create a customer."

Value Chain

Peter Drucker's third question—"What do our customers value?"—is answered through the creation of activities designed to directly serve the customer. The concept of the value chain is not new; however, its use helps to surface the choices and decisions necessary not only to serve the customer, but to help define the specific capabilities and competencies necessary to deliver those services. The value chain provides the basis for the Extended Enterprise in that all of the activities and resources that make up the value chain are identified whether or not they are contained within the scope of the formal, legal organization. Finally, the value chain forms the basis for what I call market-based transfer pricing policies.

Price-Based Costing versus Cost-Based Pricing The decisions made by senior management in establishing market-based transfer pricing policies are among the most important Governance Model implementation issues that an enterprise faces.

The issue is this: As organizations grow and add capabilities to serve their customers, those capabilities become embedded in the cost structures of the enterprise. For a while, sometimes for a long while, those costs form the basis for prices. As new competitors without the embedded costs arrive on the scene, they are able to charge lower prices without sacrificing margins. Entrenched competitors feel compelled to lower prices to maintain their customer bases but are not positioned to lower costs. The old competitors have enacted what I call "cost-based pricing" while the new competitors have adopted the corollary, "price-based costing." The new competitors have established cost structures that are well within the market prices of the old competitors. New entrants to an established industry like the airlines are good examples of the pricing-costing phenomenon. As this is being written, Southwest Airlines is being challenged by JetBlue using similar strategies employed by Southwest as a new entrant a generation ago.

Establishing a continuous tracking of competitor costs as well as constantly challenging the make-or-buy decisions associated with all of the activities of the value chain are important elements of the Governance Model. The value chain provides the framework for such tracking and analysis.

Value Chain Activities   The value chain of any enterprise consists of not more than 10 major activities within the Extended Enterprise. Those activities represent how the enterprise creates value for its customers through the linkage of competencies, capabilities, and other resources. The individual activities in the value chain represent stand-alone functions the organization may decide to "make"—that is, perform itself—or buy from outside sources that comprise the Extended Enterprise. Those stand-alone functions represent the costs of delivering value to the customer for which the customer will pay a price. The integration of the activities in the value chain creates the economic purpose of the enterprise. The more effectively the activities of the value chain fit with the needs, wants, and expectations of the customer and the more efficiently those activities are aligned with each other, the greater the value accrued to all stake owners and share owners.

Some Examples   Professor Michael Porter of Harvard, who popularized the concept of the value chain, provides many examples of its use, including Southwest Airlines, mentioned earlier. Southwest, through its focus on the needs, wants, and expectations of the budget-conscious traveler, has managed to effectively align all of the activities of the value chain—from reservations, ticketing, and boarding through in-flight service and baggage handling to the acquisition and maintenance of its aircraft. The efficiency with which Southwest has integrated such activities provides the near seamless fit between the activities, which, in turn, provides fast ground turnaround and more profitable flight operations. Southwest, at this writing, has a greater market capitalization than all of the entrenched competitors combined. JetBlue is number two in market capitalization.

Citigroup provides another example, not only of customer focus, but of alignment and fit between the activities of the value chain. The activities in the Citigroup value chain were originally designed in the 1970s to serve the specific needs of consumers versus corporations. Most other banks at that time attempted to serve all customers from one set of activities. Walter Wriston and John Reed, going against the industry norms of traditional bankers, organized separate value chains to serve:

■ Individual consumers.
■ Corporations.
■ High-net-worth individuals and trusts.

The focus, alignment, and fit between the activities of each value chain more than offset any so-called duplication of effort between the value chains as well as the loss of any potential economies of scale. The Wriston/Reed decisions of a generation ago not only formed the essence of a sustainable competitive advantage at the strategy level; those decisions also created the value at the execution level that was essential for implementation.

WellPoint Health Networks not only adopted a customer-based business model, the organization also created value chains specific to each served market or market business unit (MBU). Those value chains formed the basis for the Extended Enterprise, including:

Four Customers
1. Members
2. Payors
3. Brokers/agents (distribution channels)
4. Physicians, hospitals, and other health care professionals

Six MBUs
1. Individuals
2. Small groups
3. Key accounts
4. Major accounts
5. Special accounts
6. Government

As mentioned earlier, the WellPoint model defied industry norms in the late 1980s, as it does today. That perspective has earned WellPoint a market capitalization of over $11 billion, up from virtually zero in 1985.

The value chain decision together with the market segment decision form the basis for the execution subsystem of the Governance Model. Strategy and execution are directly linked in order that the board, executive management, and senior management be positioned to anticipate, understand, and take action around the consequences of their choices and decisions.

MANAGEMENT

As I pointed out in the preceding chapters, I am using the term "management" to illustrate:

- Roles of those having the greatest decision-making accountability and responsibility.
- Processes/activities that are often found within a particular subsystem.
- Methodologies available, including tools and techniques used to facilitate decision making.

Roles and Responsibilities

The execution subsystem of the Governance Model becomes the direct responsibility of senior management with oversight and accountability provided by executive management. The governance role of the board at this point is to assure that the accountability and responsibility are in place and working and that the organization, management process, and information systems have been implemented and are being used.

The execution subsystem of the Governance Model and the System of Governance depend on the feedback and learning attributes of Systems Thinking to implement the idea that the consequences of decisions may play out in different places and at different times from the decision itself. The System of Governance is intended to facilitate the dialogue around intended and unintended consequences of those decisions.

As we have said, the execution subsystem is all about outcomes that are knowable. The means by which such outcomes of choices and decisions become knowable is through the dialogue that must take place among senior management during the business planning process. Senior management, using the first principle of considering the whole before the parts, abandons the silo mentality and works through the possible outcomes inherent in the execution of the strategies and business plans of the Extended Enterprise.

For example, a financial services company, as a part of the examination of its value chain, made a make-or-buy decision to outsource a particular product to an organization that supplied those products to other companies. While the normal due diligence was performed at the time of the decision, an ongoing process was not put in place to monitor the creditworthiness of the supplier. Executive and senior management did not extend the consequences of their decision to the possibility that the supplier would default and not be able to fulfill its obligations. The potential consequences and their impact on the principal organization were not considered. Yet the potential for default was knowable—it had happened to others. The ultimate default of the supplier caused a liquidity crisis on the part of the principal organization, forcing a friendly takeover to avoid insolvency. The System of Governance failed as a direct result of the failures of the board, executive management, and senior management to fulfill their responsibilities, which included the anticipation and understanding of the consequences of their decisions.

Processes/Activities

As outlined in the previous chapter, the strategic direction of the Extended Enterprise is determined by a process that includes:

- Strategic assessment
- Strategic direction
- Execution planning

The Execution Loop The execution loop of the Governance Model carries forward the same process, this time at the business unit level, that defined the corporate or enterprise level. (See Figure 7.1.) The execution loop brings forward all of the feedback and learning from the strategy loop into activities of:

- Business unit assessment
- Business unit direction
- Operational planning

While the strategy loop may have looked forward for as many as five years, the execution loop is designed around a three-year rolling forward planning cycle.

The business unit assessment phase answers the question, "*What* will it take to win?" This time through the cycle, the market segmentation loop is carried forward to the analysis and decision making around customer needs, wants, and expectations as outlined earlier. Decisions around exactly how we will serve customers are made and the consequences of those

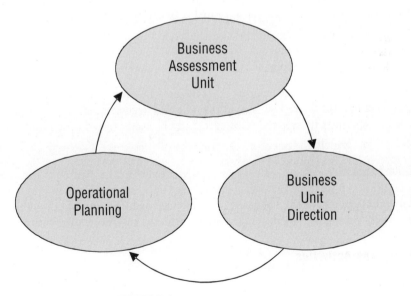

FIGURE 7.1 The Execution Loop

decisions closely examined throughout the remainder of the execution loop so that they become knowable.

The business unit direction phase answers the question, "*How* will we win?" This time the value chain analysis is carried forward around exactly what activities will be performed within the Extended Enterprise to serve the customer profitably. The decisions made during this phase of the process are closely examined for consequences throughout the value chain.

The operational planning phase is intended to answer the question, "*Who* will be responsible?" At this point in the execution loop, issues that will affect next year's operational planning and budgeting activities are addressed. The work of operational planning carries forward the activities of business planning to the operating management levels of the organization. Feedback and learning between the operational-planning phase and the business unit assessment and direction continue to test the feasibility of both strategy and execution.

Peeling the Onion A metaphor I use when describing the differences between the strategy loop and the execution loop is that of peeling an onion. Each layer of the onion looks quite similar; however, the peeling process reveals succeeding layers of insight, analysis, and depth. Concepts become clearer and better defined, notwithstanding the fact that the same tools and processes are used to peel each layer. Feedback and learning take place that facilitate the process of peeling additional layers. Perhaps more importantly, the first principle of Systems Thinking is invoked when starting with the whole and slowly moving forward through the pieces that are the layers of the onion.

Methodologies Available

Methodologies represent a critical set of tools in what I have come to call a management toolbox. They are important and necessary, and, as with most tools, they must be selected with care and are useful only in the hands of a skilled craftsman.

A Retrospective A great deal has been written over the past decade about execution of strategy. Many approaches, tools, and methodologies have emerged from both the hard and soft sciences over the period, all claiming to have the answer to making change. Among the more mechanical approaches have been:

- Reengineering and process redesign
- Activity-based costing
- Market segmentation

■ Economic modeling
■ Program and project management

These sought to provide the tools for tackling embedded bureaucracies or achieving a customer focus.

On the more qualitative side, there emerged techniques such as:

■ Change management
■ Creative destruction
■ Organizational development

These attempted to provide tools to facilitate behavioral change. Indeed, entire consulting firms and industry segments were created to deliver the tools that promised organizational success.

From the perspectives of the board, executive management, and senior management, the unlimited number of choices available presented a confusing display from which decisions were to be made. During the consulting boom years of the 1990s, the selection of tools became an issue of which brand carried the greatest promise. To further confound and complicate the decision-making process, an entire industry called Enterprise Resource Planning (ERP) emerged that promised near turnkey solutions to the complex issues of execution. Multimillion-dollar projects were undertaken in an effort to transform old-line organizations into dot-com competitors.

From a Governance Model and System of Governance perspective, the selection of methodologies, tools, and techniques added very little to the decision-making competencies of the Extended Enterprise. Systems Thinking was not at work in the selection of tools to facilitate the execution of strategy. In retrospect, I think that we will see the consulting boom years of the 1990s as more a reflection of Y2K preparation, dot-com/Internet hysteria, and the "irrational exuberance" of the stock market. There was money available, so we spent it.

Let's Drill Down Further into Business Unit Planning   As we emerge from the hangover resulting from the excesses of the 1990s and the abuses that emerged during the early 2000s, the Governance Model and the System of Governance will provide boards, executive management, and senior management with the framework and processes within which methodologies may be selected. The methodologies and tools will be chosen, as should have always been the case, based on the tasks at hand. Remember, the role of the execution loop is to provide a linkage between strategy and action. The selection of methodologies should meet that test. It is useful, then, to think about the use of methodologies as a range of tools to be applied within the context of the business planning process described earlier:

- Business unit assessment
- Business unit direction
- Operational planning

Business Unit Assessment   The choices and decisions made at the business unit level provide a focus on the customer. Since most organizations are still not truly focused on their customers, senior management has the direct responsibility for achieving such focus. Among the methodologies and tools available are those that facilitate:

- Market segmentation
- Change management

Market segmentation methodologies permit senior management to anticipate and understand which sets of customers will provide the growth and profitability required to sustain the enterprise. There are tools, consulting firms, and software available to facilitate the decisions necessary to determine which customers will provide the required focus for the enterprise. In this instance, the selection of the appropriate methodologies and tools has a narrow, well-defined purpose. Usually the leader of a business unit makes and implements the selection. The management of market risk is achieved by decisions around which set of customers becomes the focus of the enterprise.

Change management methodologies range from executive coaching to very sophisticated psychological counseling and leadership development. From a System of Governance standpoint, I believe that the most effective methodologies and tools are those which embrace the enterprise loop and create a dynamic between the human resource and the customer resource. In other words, providing the human organization with the accountability for anticipating, understanding, and taking action around the needs, wants, and expectations of a set of customers is a very powerful change management methodology. The management of the human resources risk is all about the motivation of people to serve their customers.

Business Unit Direction   Business unit direction is intended to establish the alignment and fit of the activities of the value chain with the markets and customers the enterprise chooses to serve. The concept of the value chain becoming the basis for the Extended Enterprise and the make-or-buy decisions necessary to profitably serve markets and customers is a senior management decision. The capabilities and competencies of the human organization and other enterprise resources are brought to bear in the service of customers.

The business unit leader or senior management leader charged with the accountability of matching the human and customer organization within the enterprise loop will probably select from among all of the aforementioned tools and methodologies since all are designed for particular functions and tasks. No single tool or methodology will perform all of the tasks required to achieve alignment and fit between the enterprise and its environment. The decisions to be made, including the application of Systems Thinking to those decisions in terms of consequences, feedback, and learning go a long way toward managing so-called operational risks.

Operational Planning The three-year business planning process contains, at the activity level, the operational plans and budgets for the next budget cycle of the enterprise. The business unit level of the enterprise, through the operational planning process, thinks ahead to next year to anticipate and understand the operational consequences of the choices available and the decisions contemplated. This is the phase of business planning in which operational feasibility—the reality of next year—is tested. To again quote my colleague and mentor, Peter Drucker, "All of this planning should ultimately degenerate into work." It is during this operational planning phase that business unit strategy is questioned, challenged, and possibly modified.

History teaches us that most strategy is never executed or is, at best, poorly executed. I believe that the failure of execution comes home to roost at this point in the process. All of the great ideas, wish lists, and sophisticated methodologies are useless if we are not able to translate them into action. It is at this point that an organization's competencies and capabilities to manage programs and projects meet the reality test.

From a definition standpoint, the three-year business plan consists of multiyear programs, while the one-year operational plan consists of projects that comprise the first year of those programs. All of the methodologies of market segmentation, value chain analysis, and change management take the form of programs and projects for implementation. All of the programs and projects must come together and, again applying the concepts of Systems Thinking, are tested in terms of outcomes, conflicts, inconsistencies, and redundancies.

In summary, I have found that organizations with conventional strategies may actually achieve significant competitive advantage through really effective program and project management. The reason for their success is self-evident. Most organizations do a poor job of program and project management.

CONCLUSION

The success of the Governance Model and the System of Governance is completely dependent on the rigor and discipline with which the execution subsystem is led and managed. The strategy of the enterprise is entirely at risk, as is the enterprise itself, if this dependence is not anticipated, understood, and acted upon. The choices and decisions of the board, executive management, and senior management rely completely, in terms of their outcomes, on effective execution.

The execution subsystem of the Governance Model and the System of Governance deals with outcomes that are or should be knowable. The idea that execution of strategy in most enterprises is known and knowable should reinforce the responsibility of the board, executive management, and now senior management to anticipate, understand, and take action around the rigor and discipline with which the execution subsystem of the Governance Model is undertaken. Not only are the outcomes of business plan decisions largely knowable, but the means by which we deal with those outcomes are also knowable. The application of Systems Thinking to execution provides a perspective around how we view our markets and customers, the means by which we create value, our roles and responsibilities during the process, and the techniques available to use. The execution subsystem with its available choices and decisions makes the future much more certain.

Operations—Outcomes Associated with the Present

INTRODUCTION

This chapter is intended to pick up the context of execution as well as to address the issues of day-to-day excellence in operating management. This chapter on the operations subsystem of the Governance Model and System of Governance is inserted between execution and organization, management process, and information in order that we have information around where we are going, where we are, and where we have been and the management processes for dealing with all three elements of time.

Operations is where, as Peter Drucker puts it, "all of this planning should ultimately degenerate into work." If strategy is not successfully executed, operations actually degenerates into business as usual. Without exception, strategy not effectively executed results in an enterprise which, over time, no longer fits with its environment.

With the exception of disasters and the crises that may result from those disasters, the three elements of time—where we have been, where we are, and where we are going in the near term—present outcomes that are fairly certain. The application of Systems Thinking to strategy and execution has enabled us to anticipate, understand, and be prepared to take action around the consequences of the choices available to us and the decisions we have made from among those choices. Those consequences or potential outcomes now play out in terms of operational reality—the present and the near-term future. The feedback and learning that take place within the time frame of the present enable us to make decisions to stay on course in the execution of strategy and the operation of the business.

BIG DECISIONS

Systems Thinking and the implications of cause and effect and feedback and learning define the operations subsystem and the major choices and decisions that comprise operations:

- Communications/dialogue
- Attention to detail

As usual with Systems Thinking, additional loops will become known as the process of discovery proceeds.

Communications/Dialogue

Throughout my entire career, I have been baffled by an absence of common understanding between and among people on any number of subjects. We just don't seem to listen to or hear each other. Many corporate cultures are characterized by the assertion, "He or she can finish my sentences." That may be true, but it does not mean that a clear and mutually understood meeting of the minds has taken place. What may be crystal clear to me is most likely not crystal clear to you. Having clear communications, therefore, becomes a first principle of operations. Why is communications a governance issue?

Organizations in which strategy and execution choices and decisions do not reach all the way through all levels of the firm are at risk in their efforts to continuously renew themselves. Boards, executive management, and senior management cannot create operational outcomes. Such outcomes happen only at the day-to-day transaction level of the enterprise. Operating management and the vast majority of the employees of the enterprise who do not get it and are therefore not committed will revert to business as usual (BAU) and what I have termed to be "malicious compliance." Both outcomes are dangerous. Both outcomes are the direct result of an absence of effective communications.

Business as usual is a dangerous outcome, because the external environment serves up continuous change. If we are not in day-to-day touch with such change and providing the feedback and learning to the strategy and execution loops, we become irrelevant. Clear communications around where we are going as an organization, the importance of our customers, and the relationship of our people to both issues is where effective change begins.

In the context of clear communications, it is important to reinforce the point that the only communications that are clear are those that are two-way. One-way communication is simply another way of telling people what to do or what to think. Feedback and learning do not happen. Systems Thinking is not in place. Two-way communication is the work of the System of Governance. The work is largely invisible, yet without that work, the Governance Model is not effective.

The other dangerous outcome of an ineffective communications loop is that of "malicious compliance." Individuals at all levels who feel out of the loop, whose feedback is not sought, and who are not listened to react in a very destructive way. They do what they are told to do, and no more. They do what they are told to do, even if what they are being told to do is wrong.

We have seen many examples of the results of poor communications—BAU and malicious compliance. Among the more obvious are the deterioration of customer service, product defects that go uncorrected, half-hearted efforts, and strict compliance with the rules even when the rules are wrong or out of date. Most declines in productivity and quality are the result of poor communications.

What Is the Answer?   Organizations that, in my experience, are the most effective at clear communications first of all work at it. And it is hard work. The work takes place at all levels of the enterprise, and particularly in small groups. The work, which was pointed out earlier, is the implementation of the System of Governance. Executives, managers, and supervisors at all levels take the time to bring together small groups, on an informal basis, to talk about issues that are important and to solicit feedback around what is working and what is not working. The operative word here is *empathy*—the ability of those in leadership roles to put themselves in the shoes of those they lead and to listen carefully.

I have had numerous clients over the years tell me that they don't have the time for two-way communications, that they have too much work to do. Others raise issues of confidentiality or secrecy. Still others assert that they simply don't like to talk to operating people, that they have nothing in common, or that they are not good at it. As you read these words, you know that all of these reasons are simply excuses for not doing something that is hard to do. One CEO related to me that he was sick of saying the same thing over and over. I don't blame him—I would be, too. Why would anyone enjoy saying the same thing over and over? Perhaps the unspoken answer is, it is better than listening.

The Governance Model works only when the System of Governance is in place. Since nothing happens except within the operations loop, boards, executive management, senior management, and operating management must realize that ensuring effective, two-way communications is a choice that must be decided on if the outcomes of survivability and growth are to be achieved.

Attention to Detail

I have never seen a successful organization that was not excellent at managing the details of its business. I have also seen many organizations that were good at the details but were not successful overall. The message is clear. Successfully performing the myriad of detailed operating tasks is the necessary but not sufficient attribute of a successful enterprise. The caution around attention to detail is this: Feedback and learning from doing the operating activities very well every day may cause "paralysis by analysis" in the strategy and execution subsystems of the Governance Model. Attention to detail and precision in a bottom-up way freezes the organization from the standpoint of strategy and execution, which are top-down activities. That said, the board, executive management, and senior management must be committed to operational excellence from a bottom-up perspective, while insisting on strategic and execution excellence from a top-down perspective. Both perspectives are the basis for the Governance Model and the System of Governance.

What Does Attention to Detail Mean?   There are many terms that apply to the concept of attention to detail:

- ■ "The devil is in the details"
- ■ Zero defects
- ■ Six sigma
- ■ Quality circles
- ■ Statistical quality control

From a Systems Thinking perspective, attention to detail is the input or decision while quality and productivity are the result. Feedback and learning flow back to attention to detail, reinforcing the satisfaction associated with delivering high quality. Attention to detail or operational excellence becomes a basis for competition. The equity of the enterprise's brand depends on operational excellence. Operational excellence means an intolerance for errors, mistakes, and poor quality. The Governance Model is dependent on the quality of the decisions that lead to an obsession with getting it right the first time.

Some Examples   Going back to the example of Oxford Health Plans, Inc. in the mid-1990s, the visionaries at the top lost their way in part by a failure to pay attention to the details at the bottom—operations, which, as we have said, is a bottom-up activity. When Oxford's operational processes and systems failed under the strain of volume and a largely untested new system being implemented, the failure of the company was imminent. A bottom-up attention to detail, including feedback to the strategy and execution loops, would have resulted in very different outcomes.

Conversely, attention to detail and a bottom-up philosophy of operations enabled Blue Cross of California and later WellPoint Health Networks to implement a new business model with a minimum of unintended consequences. Attention to detail is securely embedded in the culture of the company. All operating managers must be on top of their operations in order to obtain and maintain the respect of their peers, not to mention retaining their positions.

As stated earlier, the field and operating organizations of Prudential in the 1980s and early 1990s were very much in touch with the details of their businesses. The problem that ultimately surfaced was a disconnect between operations and the rest of the company. Corporate strategy did not get translated into operational action, and operational realities were not fed back to the executives charged with the responsibility of establishing strategy or planning for the execution of that strategy.

In summary, the lessons learned around the operational loop of the Governance Model and the System of Governance are deceptively simple:

- Communications/dialogue
- Attention to detail

If we apply Systems Thinking to both issues, they become the inputs or causes that drive the outcomes or results which define the performance of the enterprise. If decisions are made and reinforced that communications/dialogue and attention to detail are important, many of the surprises that we have come to know as operational risks will be either minimized or eliminated. Alternatively, the upside potential of a committed organization that pays attention to detail and provides feedback and learning to the rest of the organization is significant.

MANAGEMENT

As I previously indicated, management is intended to clarify those dimensions of who and what needs to be done to implement the operations aspects of implementation of the governance model, including:

- Roles and responsibilities
- Processes/activities
- Methodologies available

Roles and Responsibilities

The operations subsystem of the Governance Model is the primary responsibility of operating management and supervisors. While the board, executive management, and business unit management are accountable for operational results, the direct responsibility is delegated to those managers who run things on a day-to-day basis. The silos of Chapter 2 are operational when it is time to get things done.

However, Systems Thinking when applied to operational responsibilities requires that operating managers talk to each other—communicate—around the intended and unintended consequences of their decisions. An understanding at a deep level that must pervade the entire enterprise requires that action contemplated in one silo be communicated to and through all of the other silos. "Every ship does not sail on its own bottom." It should not be socially acceptable to say, "Not my problem." In fact, because every enterprise is so tightly interconnected and actions may lead to outcomes that surface at different times and spaces, the concept of "no blame" should prevail. In the words of one colleague, "You don't get fired for making a mistake; you get fired for lying."

The Governance Model relies on the System of Governance to work, to provide the feedback and learning throughout the Extended Enterprise. As related in the Prudential 1980s example, a failure in the application of Systems Thinking occurred when executive management was disconnected from operating management. This connection is a two-way street. Executive management, as a part of the System of Governance, has a direct responsibility for opening and maintaining lines of communication with operating management. Operating management has a direct responsibility to communicate not only across silos, but throughout the Extended Enterprise. Such communication is the only way that feedback and learning take place. The capability of an organization to learn, and to compete through information and knowledge, is directly dependent on the ability to anticipate, understand, and take action around the consequences of its choices and decisions. Operating management is as important a part of the feedback loop as any other participant in the loop.

Processes/Activities

As the Governance Model moves from the strategy subsystem to the execution subsystem to the operations subsystem, the processes and activities deal with greater and greater certainty. There are fewer unknowns, and most consequences of choices and decisions not only are knowable, they are known. They either have occurred, are occurring, or will occur within a short time frame.

The Operations Loop The operations loop of the Governance Model is once again a continuation of both the strategy and the execution loops (see Figure 8.1), including:

- Operations planning
- Project planning
- Departmental budgeting

The strategic planning process has moved through the business planning process to the operational planning and budgeting process. As outlined in Chapter 7 on execution, operational planning is really about developing, at an activity level, the revenue and costs for the next year. The first year of the three-year business plan sets the top-down assumptions for the bottom-up operational planning and budgeting process. Similarly, the first year of the program plans become the project plans that will be implemented during the operational planning and budgeting process. The bottom-up operational plans are developed by various levels of supervision and management of the operating units of the enterprise using the activity-level plans resulting from the execution subsystem. Feedback takes place between the two subsystems as the operating managers work to live within the assumptions of the business plans. If any operating plans, because of the bottom-up perspective, cannot fit within

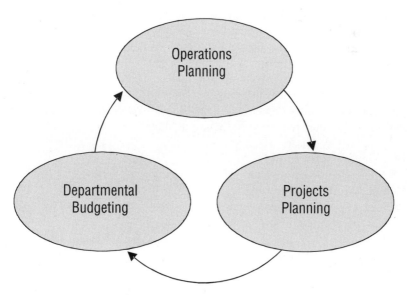

FIGURE 8.1 The Operations Loop

the constraints of the business plans, the value creation activities of the value chain are reconsidered. For example, an activity such as customer relations that may be performed in-house may be a candidate for outsourcing. Such trial-and-error, cut-and-fit, back-and-forth rationalization of the budget is an important element of the Governance Model and provides the feedback and learning that makes strategic planning, execution planning, and operational planning fit together and become stronger. An organization's ability to link all of the subsystems of the Governance Model into one seamless loop establishes the enterprise to fit within its environment and to survive and grow.

Methodologies Available

Much of the literature on the subject of risk management is focused on what is commonly called operational risk. Notwithstanding the notion that one doesn't manage an outcome, and risk is an outcome, a variety of methodologies and tools are available that may facilitate the selection of decisions from choices available. For example, going back to the conventional wisdom discussed in Chapter 2, we identified categories of tools that would avoid, mitigate, transfer, or manage and retain risk.

In view of all of our discussions around choices and decisions that enable an organization to anticipate, understand, and take action, the aforementioned categories of tools are really categories of decisions. An obvious example would be the use of insurance. Apart from the fact that most outcomes such as risk are difficult to avoid, insurance may be a tool that would mitigate, transfer, or possibly retain the consequences of our choices and decisions. Therefore, as we move forward through the generic activities or functions that comprise the operational framework of a typical enterprise, we will highlight those tools that may facilitate our decision making and therefore position us to anticipate, understand, and take action around the consequences of our choices and decisions. The generic operational activities that we will discuss include:

- Human resources
- Marketing, sales, and service
- Operationals and technology
- Innovation and renewal
- Alliances/suppliers and network partners
- Finance

As we will see in the next chapter, these categories also align for the most part with our discussion on organization, management process, and information.

Human Resources As discussed in Chapter 3 when introducing the enterprise loop, we place the human organization in the position of driving the value creation activities of the enterprise. Our available choices and the decisions we make enable the Governance Model and the System of Governance to work, or not work. There can be no more important decisions made by an enterprise than the decisions around people. The ability of the enterprise to attract, develop, and retain the right people—that is, people who fit within the enterprise and its environment and who represent the embedded knowledge of the organization—will determine the competitive success of the enterprise. The choices or decision-making criteria that are available to organizations and that will ultimately define the types of people available to the enterprise include:

■ Selection criteria
■ Shared vision and values
■ Culture and accepted behavior
■ Systems of recognition and reward
■ Leadership and management models
■ Development and training

As we will see in the next chapter, employee knowledge and satisfaction provide the initial set of leading indicators that reveal the overall health profile of the organization.

The operations subsystem of the Governance Model is where the reality of people decisions really comes home to roost. Senior executives may "talk the talk" about the importance of people; but it is the day-to-day operating management and supervisors who must walk that talk. From a governance standpoint, the board, executive management, and senior management must all be aware of and actively engaged in the development of the human resources.

Some Examples "Walking the talk" is, of course, all about what we do or don't do, versus what we say. The System of Governance is really the behavior of the leadership at all levels. Within the System of Governance, the leadership is watched every day in terms of its decisions and the consistency of those decisions with espoused values. An organization whose values preach teamwork, mutual respect, and cooperation but is quick to find fault, assign blame, and publicly criticize will have very few of the stated values in actual practice. Organizations that blame the messenger or the bearer of bad news will receive little feedback, and the learning will make certain that keeping quiet is the preferred survival technique. From a Governance Model standpoint, boards, executive management, and senior management have to be sufficiently in touch with operations to make certain that the lessons learned of communications and attention to detail are being carried out in ways that facilitate the feedback and learning, not inhibit them. High-quality operational decisions occur only in an atmosphere in which the decisions that lead to good enterprise-wide outcomes are rewarded and learning takes place from those decisions that create unintended consequences.

Marketing, Sales, and Service   Market segmentation decisions made in the execution subsystem directly impact the customers to which we market, sell, and serve in the operational subsystem. From a governance and risk standpoint, the choices and decisions made at one level directly impact operational decisions concerning customer selection and retention. Those operational decisions, of course, result in outcomes such as credit risk, ethical risk, conflicts of interest, and regulatory risk. For example, if we have selected a market segment characterized as having high credit risk, an operational decision must be made around the specific characteristics of the individuals we choose to serve. If we are dealing with a market segment that may consist of organizations or individuals of questionable character, we must also be careful in selecting our customers at a very specific or individual level; and finally, if we are selling to individuals who don't need, don't want, or cannot pay for our product or service, we run into regulatory risks, not to mention the risks to our organizational values. All of these examples highlight the cause and effect, feedback and learning attributes of our Governance Model.

An effective human organization creates the customers it chooses to serve. As mentioned earlier, Peter Drucker's definition of the purpose of the organization is to create a customer. In most enterprises, the people select the external and internal customers they choose to serve.

The strategy and execution choices and decisions translate into the specific individuals to be served by the enterprise. The operational choices and decisions, as was the case with human resources choices and decisions, lead to specific selection criteria. The decisions an enterprise makes around the selection of its customers not only are a reflection of the people who are applying the selection criteria but actually anticipate, understand, and take action around the range of outcomes associated with serving that individual customer, including:

■ Ethical character
■ Credit worthiness
■ Conflicts of interest

Some Examples   Loose hiring practices are a clear human resources decision. That decision may result in a lack of rigor in selecting customers who will help to sustain and grow the enterprise. Marginal quality hiring choices set the tone for the nature of the customers an organization is willing to accept. The outcomes of the human organization often determine the outcomes of the customer base. This point on quality has nothing to do with the economic or social status of either the human organization or the customers attracted to the enterprise. A case in point is the subprime lending business. The employees who select customers with low incomes or poor credit histories create successful outcomes by being very capable in selecting customers. The employees, at the operational level, know their customers and know when to lend them money and when not to lend them money. The successful participants in the subprime lending industry attract individuals who know when not to make loans. The successful employee in this industry understands that making a loan that can't be repaid hurts everyone.

Successful marketing, sales, and service decisions lead to outcomes that fit the customers to the capabilities of the enterprise. The better the fit between the needs, wants, and expectations of the markets and customers we serve with the capabilities of the enterprise, the fewer the unintended consequences and risks.

Operations and Technology For the purpose of this discussion on the operations and technology aspects of the operational subsystem of the Governance Model, we have linked the two activities together because it is very difficult to separate them. Most operations and technology issues in most Extended Enterprises are tightly linked in terms of cause and effect, space and time. By operations and technology, we mean those activities, including people and processes, that carry out most of the value creation efforts of the enterprise. Indeed, operations and technology, when done well, present a seamless linkage between the customers and suppliers of the organization.

When things go wrong in the day-to-day activities of the Extended Enterprise, we often refer to an operational failure. In fact, operational risk ranks very high in any conventional assessment of risk. When we apply Systems Thinking to the operations and technologies of the enterprise, it becomes clear that the vast majority of the so-called operational failures were, in fact, the unintended consequences of a decision made elsewhere in the Extended Enterprise, often at a very different time.

Rhetorical Question To this day, nearly 50 years after the first commercial availability of computer systems, the operational consequences of poor implementation decisions are still being blamed for operational failures. Technical glitches still occur in unexpected places long after systems are presumably debugged. The reality is that the number of permutations that are possible, even within the most straightforward processes, is infinite. So, too, are the unexpected consequences of such operational and technology failures. The question is this: If such failures are really routine, why aren't they treated in a routine way? Why don't back up processes routinely kick in and resume processing? I believe that the answer to the rhetorical question is simply that in a world of lateral thinking, such failures are treated as surprises. They aren't supposed to happen. In the world of Systems Thinking, the likelihood of an unplanned operational outcome is very high and therefore anticipated, understood, and acted upon. The feedback and learning that take place will continue to build in redundancies and self-correcting mechanisms, while all along being completely aware that such operations and technology failures not only are knowable, they are known, expected, and built into the operational processes of the enterprise.

ERP Failure   Operations and technology choices and decisions within the Governance Model are ideal examples of the differences between traditional lateral thinking and Systems Thinking. Lateral thinking has led to systems complexity that goes beyond human comprehension in terms of what can go wrong. The massive failures of many so-called Enterprise Resource Planning (ERP) systems, notwithstanding the billions spent on their development and implementation, are a case in point. Failures of systems of such complexity not only are routine, they are knowable and are virtually certain.

From the governance and risk perspective at the board, executive management, and senior management levels, how should this nearly certain outcome of operational and technology risk be dealt with? First, the prospect of implementing a $100 million plus system is clearly a board issue in any corporation. Further, the unanticipated consequences of such a decision must be played out throughout the Governance Model. That is, the strategic, execution, and operations consequences of the decision must be anticipated, understood, and acted upon. The Governance Model is the framework to be used for such decision making. The use of the Governance Model as a decision making framework may still result in the decision to move ahead with a major systems implementation; however, the scope and approach to that implementation will reflect a new reality of how to proceed with a minimum of unintended consequences.

To be certain, there are risk assessment tools and methodologies available that may help to classify possible outcomes and indeed to test an organization's compliance with known areas of potential risks. Internal and external audit organizations have developed elaborate checklists and procedures for examining the operations and technology activities of an organization, and, indeed, such approaches are valuable and produce important results.

Some Examples   Specific examples of the types of activities undertaken by organizations to anticipate and understand the nature of the operations and technology risks that may be potentially encountered include:

- Enterprise Resource Planning (ERP) controls, assessment, and design.
- Data quality controls
- Attack and penetration security studies.
- Package selection and implementation.
- Infrastructure security services.
- E-business assurance.

Such efforts, as economists say, are the necessary, but not sufficient, contributors to the management of known and knowable risks.

Finally, operations and technology choices and decisions and related outcomes need not be classified as operational risk. One need not study operational activities and attempt to assess what might go wrong or to understand the so-called risks associated with operations and technology. Rather, it is more appropriate to recognize that failure in any complex system is both routine and certain and that the appropriate choices and decisions are to provide backup and redundancy as a matter of course. What went wrong at Xerox? Many things went wrong, as is the case with all significant missteps. Among Xerox's mistakes, however, was the failure of the board and executive management to provide the operating organization with the new ideas necessary for survival and to provide the research organization with the reality of anticipating and understanding the needs of the customer.

As this book is being written, Hewlett-Packard is in the process of integrating its merger with Compaq Computer. The future of the combined firms is obviously not known or perhaps even knowable. What we can anticipate, however, is that the 60-year edge that Hewlett-Packard maintained around unique solutions to customer problems and the culture of engineering is at risk. Hewlett-Packard, seeking the ever-elusive economies of scale that presumably come with size, runs the very big risk of losing the fundamental culture that made it a great company. The board and executive management have their work cut out for them; but the anticipation and understanding of the long-run consequences of their choices and decisions are their work.

Innovation and Renewal   Innovation and renewal are more a part of the System of Governance than of the framework of the Governance Model. Innovation and renewal are a state of mind more than a hardwired methodology. Yet, enterprise growth and survival are direct outcomes of the capacity and capability of the organization for renewal. Choices available and decisions made around an organization's capability to learn and develop customer solutions before the customer recognizes the need for such solutions determine the future of the enterprise.

Innovation and renewal are discussed as a component of the operations subsystem of the Governance Model because it is at the operations level of the enterprise that actual contact is made with the external environment. Feedback and learning that occur as a result of the outcomes of choices and decisions provide the basis for innovation and renewal. In effect, applied research is a direct result of such feedback and learning.

The application of Systems Thinking to innovation and renewal is centered on an organization's choices and decisions for:

- Research and Development (R&D) investments
- New products/services
- Pilot projects/experiments
- Patents or valuable formulas
- Uses of new technologies
- Continuous improvement
- Different forms of organization

In addition, an organization's capacity for cultivating new ideas, from leadership concepts to strategic alliances, encourages decisions that provide outcomes to assure the future of the enterprise.

The organizational feedback and learning that take place as a result of vigorous innovation activities enable an enterprise to constantly reinvent itself and remain relevant in its markets and to its customers. The risk implication for an organization that makes decisions that do not foster innovation and renewal is the question of survival.

An Example   Finally, some good news. IBM a decade ago was on the slippery slope to oblivion. Big Blue, never an innovator, was fast losing its capacity to renew itself. Lou Gerstner and his team not only defied most external experts by not breaking the company up as had been widely speculated, they also breathed a new life and vigor into a massive risk-averse culture. By keeping the science and technology at the forefront, IBM actually used innovation as a strategy for renewal of the company. While IBM has clearly followed the trend of information technologies into services (particularly with the acquisition of PwC Consulting from PricewaterhouseCoopers to form IBM Business Consulting Services), new technology breakthroughs have kept the company on the leading edge of innovation. IBM's board and executive management clearly understand that if they do not achieve excellence in technology, their service businesses will be implementing the technologies developed by others.

Innovation and renewal comprise the lifeblood of the Extended Enterprise. The Governance Model provides a framework for boards and executive management to keep asking the question, "What are we doing to stay ahead?" Sheer size is not the answer to that question.

Alliances/Suppliers and Network Partners   We live in a world of networks. The present Web-enabled, Internet-connected environment presents innovative organizations with an infinite variety of choices, decisions, risks, and rewards. Our environment has, seemingly all at once, become global and interconnected in ways that are only now beginning to unfold. The buffers of time, space, and distance are gone forever. The networked world in which we live and do business is a direct result of the science that underlies the discipline of Systems Thinking.

The application of Systems Thinking to alliances/suppliers and network partners in the new world presents a natural way, if not the only way, of looking at decisions and risks across an infinite variety of participants. We are all connected and provide feedback to and among each other. In fact, the concept of the Extended Enterprise, the subject of Chapter 4, is in fact a network—a network that consists of, among others, alliances/suppliers and network partners. Just as we face choices and make decisions around activities that are supposedly within our control, we face day-to-day operational choices and decisions, the consequences of which are enormous for the survival of the enterprise. Here are just a few of the choices we face:

- Quality of supplier's products and services.
- Availability and access to information.
- Viability and reputation of suppliers and counterparties.
- Reliability and stability of outsource or shared service providers.
- Integrity and quality of databases.
- Security of software and software providers.
- Security of public networks.
- Reliability of suppliers' vendors.

In a world of networks, the impact of a failure of an alliance/supplier or a network partner can have devastating consequences.

Some Examples   The failure of a supplier of financial products to a highly rated mutual insurance company and its subsidiary resulted in a liquidity crisis for the parent company. Ultimately, to avoid some draconian form of rehabilitation by the state insurance commission, the parent and the subsidiary were sold. The board, executive management, and, in this case, operating management never contemplated the consequences of such a failure. The silo organization understood only the parts of the supplier relationship, not the whole, and certainly not the fit of the Extended Enterprise with the external environment.

In Chapter 4 I presented the examples of the aerospace and defense industry and the automobile industry as cases that illustrated the Extended Enterprise.

Those examples are once again relevant at the operations level when considering the role of alliances/suppliers and network partners. The board, executive management, and operating management are charged with the *responsibility* of anticipating, understanding, and in the case of operations, taking action around the consequences of real or potential failure at any point in the network. The word *responsibility* is stressed here to place emphasis on the fact that the quality, safety, and reliability of the end product—the airplane or automobile as a system—are the responsibility of the board and executive and operating management. Neither the board nor management may avoid that responsibility by blaming the system failure on a faulty component or subsystem supplied by a network partner. There is no blame. Everyone is responsible.

The evaluation and monitoring of the decisions and risks associated with alliances/suppliers and network partners must be continuous to be effective. Again, the feedback characteristics of network models provide the information necessary for making decisions and understanding risk. The quality of the decisions, based on information that is not only knowable but known, will determine the degree to which the enterprise will capture the power of networks and secure the benefits of rewards associated with timely and reliable information.

Legal and Regulatory Compliance   The outcomes of many of our choices and decisions must be anticipated, understood, and acted upon with a view toward our regulators, rating agencies, and the legal community. The Governance Model places the activity of legal and regulatory compliance within the operational subsystem of the Governance Model because it is through the day-to-day operating choices and decisions that we create outcomes that subject the enterprise to unexpected consequences. Legal and regulatory compliance choices and decisions are also framed in operational terms because the risks associated with being out of compliance are certain and known.

As discussed in earlier chapters, the Tone at the Top sets the stage for much of the behavior within the System of Governance, but none more evident than around legal and regulatory compliance. Attitudes such as, "If it is legal, it must be ethical," and attempts to wink at the rules permeate the actions taken throughout the enterprise. Attempting to fix or shift blame establishes a culture that avoids taking responsibility. Yet taking responsibility for doing the right thing is at the heart of the concept of governance.

I've worked with many organizations that operate in regulated industries and have never seen one institution that was successful over the long
run that also evaded compliance responsibilities. The ethical tone at the
top set the standard for every operational decision. The successful companies, in my experience, do not ask whether a proposed decision is legal;
they ask whether it is right. Successful companies don't tweak the rules to
get under the radar of compliance; they operate in a way that there are no
decisions made that if exposed to close public scrutiny would not pass the
test of pride.

Being compliant is a necessary but not sufficient test of good governance. Checklists, sign-offs, representations, and certifications will not
guarantee ethical and legal behavior. What will be accomplished by the
new rules is an increasing awareness that choices and decisions must receive close scrutiny at all levels. It will no longer be, and actually never
was, enough for a board member or executive to offer the excuse "I didn't
know" or "They didn't tell me."

Finance   Finance is the last of the operations subsystems to be discussed
for several reasons:

- The results or outcomes of most enterprise activities have financial
  outcomes, sooner or later.
- Financial outcomes are usually considered at the end of the strategy or
  execution planning process when it is determined whether such plans
  meet preestablished targets.
- The financial activity is a negative feedback loop that serves as a governor or regulator of other activities.

In many ways, the finance activity establishes the ground rules by
which other activities within the enterprise play the game. Also, when we
consider the enterprise loop (Figure 3.2), the goals part of the loop refers to
the targets established by the enterprise, which represent those financial
outcomes required for survival and the creation of shareholder value. Finally, in the left-brain, quantitative world in which most of us live, most
decisions take on financial implications, whether or not those outcomes
may be really quantified.

Our task in this section of the operations subsystem of the Governance
Model is to present the choices and decisions that have a more direct bearing on financial outcomes, including:

- Protection against potential losses.
- Funding the enterprise.
- Limits to growth.

Protection against Loss   It is interesting to note how often issues of risk management degenerate into the subject of insurance. Indeed, the risk management function of many companies is basically the insurance department.

Obviously, the protection of the tangible and intangible property of the enterprise must be protected against loss through insurance or guard dogs. Fires, terrorism, flood, earthquakes, theft, errors and omissions, and all forms of specialized loss must be protected against in the most efficient and economical manner.

Other forms of potential loss, including foreign currency fluctuations, interest rate changes, and commodity prices, to name just a few, must be efficiently and economically protected against as well.

The cause-and-effect implications of using the insurance and capital markets to protect against potential loss is really where the terms avoid, mitigate, transfer, or manage and retain risk originate. These are important choices, and the decisions that emanate from such choices have a direct bearing on at least a portion of the financial outcomes of the enterprise. The board and executive management would not be exercising their fiduciary duties were they not concerned with the protection against potential losses.

Funding the Enterprise   Systems Thinking when applied to the choices and related decisions around how the enterprise is funded presents challenging survival and growth issues for the board and executive management. Choices available range from private equity to mutual or cooperative societies to debt to some form of public ownership. The enterprise loop and the environment loop, taken together, provide the context and framework for such choices. As stated in Chapter 3 around the discussion of the two loops, capital markets and competition provide the signals that enable the board and executive management to anticipate, understand, and take action around the consequences of the decisions taken to fund the enterprise. Within the enterprise loop, the human and customer subsystems also provide important signals.

An Example   An example of how all of these signals come together and drive the funding decision is Kaiser Permanente. Kaiser is a nonprofit organization that is really owned by the citizens of the states in which it operates. Kaiser is also an integrated health system inasmuch as the Kaiser members or customers have the majority of their health care needs fully covered by the Kaiser hospitals and the Kaiser health care providers. In Systems Thinking terms, Kaiser is a one-loop system.

During the 1990s, the environment loop, including the competition and capital markets subloop, undoubtedly sent signals to the Kaiser board and executive management to fund the enterprise with public money. There was ample available capital, and the public companies such as United Health and WellPoint were creating significant shareholder value. At the same time, the human and customer components of the enterprise loop were sending even more powerful signals around the importance of a nonprofit organization as a health care delivery system. The Kaiser beliefs and values outweighed the opportunities and pressures of the external environment. The decision was and is to remain a nonprofit system.

I use the Kaiser example and the leadership of Dr. David Lawrence to illustrate the principle that the choices and decisions around funding the enterprise, if not considered within the framework of the enterprise and environment Loops, the Governance Model, and System of Governance, may produce consequences far beyond who owns the enterprise.

This discussion on funding the enterprise is not intended to describe all of the pros and cons of alternative choices and decisions, but rather to point out the requirement on the part of the board and executive management to anticipate and understand the consequences of their decisions.

Limits to Growth   As stated earlier, the finance activity is a negative feedback loop that serves as a governor or regulator of other activities. There are two ways in which the finance activity fulfills this function within the Governance Model:

1. Targets for the growth of revenue and profitability.
2. Annual operating budget.

Left to their own devices, with no constraints, the human and the customer aspects of the enterprise loop would run the wheels off of the enterprise. If prices and costs and the resulting profitability challenges were not considered, the result would be chaos. Targets for growth and profitability, which are the financial outcomes of strategy, provide the upward and downward limits within which strategy is to be developed. The Governance Model requires that the board and executive management establish such targets as well as anticipate, understand, and take action around the consequences of such targets being achieved or not achieved.

A good example of the board and executive management applying the Governance Model and the System of Governance to the subject of targets is that of executive compensation. Regardless of the form of such compensation, the board must be assured that both growth and profitability must be within ranges set at the beginning of the year, long before payouts are awarded at the end of the year. (For discussion of executive compensation in the context of establishing corporate objectives, see Chapter 6, "Strategy—Outcomes Associated with the Future.")

The annual operating budget is another tool that may be used by the board, executive management, business unit management, and operating supervision to keep the enterprise in bounds. Within the context of the Governance Model, the budget is the final decision made by the board prior to the launch of a new year. The budget process does not drive the strategy or execution subsystems, but it does reduce those decisions to their final terms and establish who will be responsible for taking the action necessary to assure that actual outcomes are within the ranges determined during the budgeting process.

In summary, the finance activity of the operations subsystem should be the last consideration within the framework of the Governance Model. The finance activity is not about the management of risk. The finance activity is designed to provide the boundaries within which the enterprise may grow.

CONCLUSION

The operations subsystem of the Governance Model is of equal importance to the board and to executive management, as are the strategy and execution subsystems. While the board and executive management may not and probably should not take an active role in the management of the operational activities, they are accountable for the results of those activities. That accountability is exercised by the board and executive management ensuring that the appropriate management processes are in place and are being employed. The board and executive management may not say, "We didn't know" or "We weren't told." Period!

Organization, Management Process, and Information

INTRODUCTION

The final subsystem of the Governance Model provides the connection and feedback mechanisms between the other three subsystems of the Governance Model. The organization, management process, and information subsystem is really an integral part of each of the other three subsystems. I have depicted it separately in order to provide focus, but the components of organization, management process, and information are found throughout the tangible Governance Model and the intangible System of Governance.

For the purposes of this discussion around organization, management process, and information, I will focus on how each topic relates to governance decision making and risk.

It is important to note that the three topics represent a system—the whole. These are not separate subjects to be addressed and implemented in a fragmented way, but rather they are so tightly connected that a piecemeal approach simply will not work.

BIG DECISIONS

Systems Thinking and the implication of cause and effect, feedback and learning define the organization, management process, and information subsystems and the major choices and decisions that comprise the subsystem:

- One information system for the Extended Enterprise.
- Keep it simple.
- Precision is not required.
- Fast-track implementation.

The implementation of organization, management process, and information is really a learning exercise. I have yet to see a situation in which an entire system of management is designed and implemented in one step *and worked*. We all learn by doing, by personal hands-on involvement, and by trial and error. Well-done systems of management take years to become fully functional and baked into the fabric of the enterprise. They would never be fully functional without continuous learning and improvement.

FRAMEWORK FOR THINKING ABOUT ORGANIZATION, MANAGEMENT PROCESS, AND INFORMATION

I will use the Governance Model as a reference within which to frame the issues of organization, management process, and information. The Governance Model is, of course, a model for decision making and for dealing with the consequences of decisions. Rather than attempting to describe all of the potential aspects of the subject, I will discuss only those which relate to the choices and decisions at each level of the Governance Model.

Organization—and Decision Making

In this section, I have developed a generalized model of a wide variety of organizations that I have studied over the years. Of course, any specific organization will vary to some degree from this model; however, the main components, including roles and responsibilities of various units, should be present.

Board of Directors   As I have previously indicated, the role of the board is the survival and growth of the enterprise for the benefit of its share owners and stakeholders. The board fulfills that role within the Governance Model through its involvement in the major decisions undertaken at a strategy level and through its monitoring of the decision-making processes throughout the enterprise. This role of the board in major decisions and decision making assumes that the members of the board are in compliance with the Sarbanes-Oxley Act of 2002 and all of the rules and regulations emanating from the SEC, Nasdaq, and other bodies. This discussion of the role of the board is intended to highlight the means by which the board may anticipate, understand, and take action on the consequences of the decisions made throughout the Extended Enterprise.

During the course of my research and to confirm or refine my thinking on the roles and responsibilities of boards of directors, I called on Frances Hesselbien, chairman of the board of the Peter F. Drucker Foundation in New York. I have known Frances since my days at the Drucker School, having worked with her to establish the Drucker Library at Claremont Graduate University. Frances is a gifted writer and speaker on the subjects of leadership and governance, in particular, nonprofit organizations. Frances' history of nonprofit leadership can be traced back to her roots as CEO of the Girl Scouts of the USA, as well as her more recent service as a facilitator on leadership at the U.S. Army War College. Frances' terms are a little different from mine; however, when it comes to the roles and responsibilities of the board, her meaning and mine are in accord. According to Frances, the board has three roles:

1. Strategic planning, including the board's vision and mission, major strategies, and overarching goals.
2. Determination of major policies.
3. Oversight.

There is very little difference between Frances' thinking and mine when her thoughts are placed within the Governance Model and the System of Governance. When discussing the role of executive management, Frances is equally direct. Management is accountable to the board for the work of the organization.

Our interview ended with a request from Frances that I inform directors and senior executives: "Just do what you are called to do. It is never a job."

I was also most fortunate to have spent some time discussing governance and risk with David Blake, a professor in the Graduate School of Management at the University of California at Irvine. David, who sits on a number of boards, had several observations regarding what he calls "boards that work," They:

■ Tend toward activism, but do not become meddlesome.
■ Are alert and make suggestions.
■ Act in an advisory and counseling role.
■ Serve as teachers.

When I asked David why people do board service of any kind he responded, "People want to help something to flourish, to make a contribution." I received almost the exact response from everyone with whom I spoke.

Our conversation turned to risk, and he replied to questions around risk management, "One may not manage risk, but one can manage for risk." To me, that is a helpful perspective that I incorporated earlier in this book.

Finally, when we discussed the amount of time contributed by board members of even relatively small enterprises, David's response was four to five hours per week. David also asserted that board members who take their role seriously and make the commitment of their time and talent are seriously underpaid.

As this book enters its final stages of editing, the long-standing issue of separation of the roles of chairman of the board and chief executive officer is once again under serious discussion, this time by the Conference Board. As reported in the *Wall Street Journal* on January 10, 2003,

> *The Commission on Public Trust and Private Enterprise suggested a set of what were called "best practices" dealing with governance, share owner relations, and the accounting industry. The so-called problem that such best practices were intended to solve was that of "strong CEOs [who] appear to have executed a dominant influence over their boards, often stifling the efforts of directors to play the central oversight role needed to ensure a healthy system of corporate governance."*

Once again, corporate governance seems related to power, not decision making. It is not at all clear to me that splitting the power does anything to improve decision making; rather, it diffuses and complicates the issue of responsibility for effective decisions, particularly from an investor perspective. In my view, if a CEO is so dominant and intimidating to his or her fellow board members, the board needs to deal with that issue, not to further complicate matters by splitting power and setting up independent governance processes. I sincerely hope that our "best practices" address core issues rather than symptoms.

The Governance Committee   Decisions and decision making at the board level may most appropriately fall into the newly emerging committee of the board—the governance committee. The governance committee is becoming a reality as mandated by the New York Stock Exchange and as recommended by Nasdaq. Heretofore, the idea behind the charters of most governance committees mainly dealt with nominating processes, regulatory compliance, and board evaluation. Those are important activities and should be part of the charter of the governance committee; however, if governance is really all about choices and decisions, I believe the charter should be expanded to include the monitoring of the Governance Model and the System of Governance throughout the enterprise.

The expanded charter of the governance committee should include:

- Board qualifications and selection process (nominating committee).
- Evaluations of the board and executive management, using the template of the Governance Model as the basis for such evaluation.

■ Succession planning.
■ Involvement in the long-term strategic decisions of the Extended Enterprise, including the potential consequences of such decisions.
■ Oversight of the decision-making processes throughout the Extended Enterprise.
■ Interface with a chief risk officer, if such position is created within the enterprise.

In short, the governance committee is the ideal organizational unit to work with executive management in dealing with those relatively few strategic decisions that make a difference in the survival and growth of the organization. The governance committee can also assure that appropriate decision-making practices are in place throughout the enterprise.

Executive Management—Policy Committee   Within the context of the Governance Model, executive management is charged with the accountability and responsibility of working with the board of directors to implement the strategic subsystem of the model. Executive management, one or two of whom may also serve on the board, comprises the senior policy-level executives in the enterprise and constitutes what I will call the policy committee. Executive management is charged with establishing the strategic direction of the organization through the decision-making process and through the feedback and learning that take place reflecting the consequences of those decisions. The implementation of the Governance Model and the System of Governance is the responsibility of executive management. The activities established within the strategy subsystem of the Governance Model are actually carried out by the relatively few, perhaps less than 10, members of the policy committee. This is an important point, because the members of the policy committee not only must be accountable and responsible for the decisions and their consequences but must "own" these decisions. By "own," I mean they need to be deeply involved not only in the process, but in the decisions and their potential consequences as well. This ownership and involvement apply to those decisions to pursue a course of action as well as those decisions not to do something. A decision is a decision.

Senior Management—Executive Committee   Senior management, those executives who are responsible for business units, activities, or major functions, is responsible and accountable for the execution subsystem of the Governance Model. The business unit planning activities are carried out by the executive committee and are designed to carry forward the decisions made at the strategy level into the actual value creation activities at the execution level. The executive committee makes decisions around execution in much the same way that the policy committee makes decisions around strategy. Not only is the executive committee deeply involved in the process, they "own" the decisions and the consequences of those decisions.

To be more specific, the executive committee usually includes, in addition to the heads of the business units, the leaders of the following functions or activities:

- Human resources
- Marketing
- Technology/operations/facilities
- Finance
- Legal and regulatory compliance
- Product development and distribution

This may also be the level at which the chief risk officer (CRO) reports. Indeed, it may be the CRO who monitors and tracks the decisions and decision-making process throughout the Governance Model.

How Does the Process Really Work? In a typical organization as characterized in Figure 2.2 the silos represent real barriers to understanding the results of decisions arrived at in different times and places. The companion issues of coordination, cooperation, and communication are critical to achieving the required anticipation and understanding of the outcomes of the decisions made at the strategy level. The question is how to achieve the required coordination, cooperation, and communication without creating more silos. It has been my experience that the creation of interdisciplinary task forces or cross-functional committees creates its own problem of complexity. Instead, I have found it useful for the leaders of the business units, as a part of the business planning process, to carry forward the critical decisions to all functions and activities of the Extended Enterprise. Those functional leaders may then evaluate the consequences of the business planning decisions on their own operations and provide feedback to the business unit leaders. The functional leaders, in turn, create programs and projects that take into consideration all of the decisions made by the business unit leaders.

An Example The development of one- to three-year business plans is the direct responsibility of the executive committee as outlined in the execution subsystem. It is the job of those senior managers to figure out how their decisions are anticipated, understood, and acted upon throughout the Extended Enterprise. It is also their job to make the consequences of such decisions at least knowable. Clearly, those senior managers cannot simply develop their business plans and expect that those decisions will be successfully implemented. At the same time, the business planning process cannot become so cumbersome and so people-intensive that the clarity and responsibility of the decisions for implementation are lost or defused. "Too many cooks," so to speak.

One organization with which I am familiar charges the senior executives to work through the issues of market segmentation and the determination of activities value chain—remember the Big Decisions of Chapter 7, "Execution"—with the leaders of product development, distribution, and the services that are shared by all of the business units. Instead of forming teams with representation from those various functions and activities, the business unit leaders, in effect, acquire the products, distribution, and shared services necessary to serve their market segments. The business unit leaders, according to company policy, make the Big Decisions found in the execution subsystem with the other senior executives of the enterprise. This relatively straightforward policy pinpoints responsibility and accountability directly where it belongs without the need for elaborate multidisciplined groups of people attempting to come together to develop the business plan.

It is important to highlight the decision-making process that took place around the aforementioned policy statement. The policy committee, as the senior decision-making body within the enterprise, made a strategic decision to hold the business unit leaders accountable for the profitability of the enterprise. Because the organization is highly integrated—that is, product development, distribution, and corporate activities are shared by all business units—the business unit leaders work in an environment in which they are not directly responsible for either revenue or costs. The organizational decision to hold the business unit leaders accountable for bringing together revenue and costs created a high degree of clarity around who was responsible for what decisions. That clarity enables the business unit leaders to acquire the products, distribution, and services necessary to serve their customers at market prices and at market costs.

Operating Management—Operations Committee As stated in Chapter 8, "Operations—Outcomes Associated with the Present," the Big Decisions center around attention to detail and communications/dialogue. Operations management has the organizational responsibility for getting things right—the first time. While accountability may reside with executive or senior management, the responsibility buck stops with operations management. By the time decisions are worked through the first two levels of the Governance Model, the potential consequences—outcomes and risks—should be known. It is the job of operations management to make certain that the consequences of strategic and execution decisions are surfaced from an operations perspective and either dealt with or fed back in order that those strategic and execution decisions are reexamined. Operations management, if it is doing its job within the Governance Model, has the direct responsibility for providing such feedback.

An Example   I worked with one multibillion-dollar service company that embarked on a series of successful, relatively small acquisitions in related fields. The due diligence process worked quite well throughout the Governance Model. A potential acquisition surfaced that would double the size of the company and make it number one in size within its industry sector. The decision-making process, which was really a due diligence process, moved from the board of directors through executive and senior management with the conclusion that the acquisition was "a stretch, but doable." As the decision moved to operations management, the unintended consequences began to surface. Operations management, in examining the details of integration, concluded that as a result of the size, complexity, and culture of the operations of the potential acquisition, "We would end up looking like them." That conclusion was devastating. It was also true. The successful acquiring company would have been so diluted by the relatively unsuccessful acquisition that the character of the acquiring company would be lost. The conclusion was fed back to executive management and the board with the result that the acquisition was abandoned. A decision *not to do* something is often more important than a decision *to do* something. Operations management had fulfilled its responsibilities. The board, executive management, and senior management had fulfilled their accountabilities. The Governance Model and the System of Governance had performed their functions.

Management Process

I briefly touched on management process in the preceding chapters on the Governance Model. This discussion focused not on process for the sake of process or control but on processes related to decision making. Strategy dealt with those processes for handling the future unknowns, and execution dealt with the knowable outcomes, while operations dealt with the known results. This section on management process carries forward the ideas around decision making at the strategy, execution, and operations levels to the continuous processes required to track performance compared to plans developed at those three levels. The continuous monitoring of actual performance and the decisions required to stay on track are at least as important an aspect of the Governance Model as the annual planning cycle. In fact, it is the continuous monitoring of cause and effect that enables feedback and learning to take place. Systems Thinking is a daily, minute-by-minute perspective across the Extended Enterprise.

It has been my experience that once the strategic, execution, and operations plans have been put in place, the real work of continuous feedback and learning happens. Keeping on course is a real-time activity on the part of all participants—from the board to operating supervision. The System of Governance, the behavioral model of the enterprise, defines *how* the people of the organization work together to make the necessary course correction decisions to achieve the promised outcomes and avoid or minimize the unintended consequences of those decisions. The System of Governance, which shadows the Governance Model, also functions in terms of *who*, and requires that the enterprise come together at the various levels to constantly learn from and with each other about what is and is not working. These levels are:

- Board of directors—governance committee.
- Executive management—policy committee.
- Senior management—executive committee.
- Operating management—operations committee.

Open, collegial, shared dialogue and trust are at the essence of this System of Governance. The management processes by which the System of Governance is carried out may include:

- The governance committee of the board of directors,
- The policy committee or body of the enterprise charged with accountability for the development of strategy.
- The executive committee or body charged with accountability for the execution of strategy.
- The senior management group assigned the responsibility for operations.

Board of Directors—Governance Committee The governance committee, or whatever board level organization is charged with working with management on key strategic decisions, must have an in-depth understanding of the enterprise and the industry in order to be effective partners in decision making. The governance committee, perhaps through the efforts of a lead director or nonexecutive chairman, works with executive management on no less than a quarterly basis to monitor the status of the strategic decisions made as part of the strategic planning process. As we will see from the discussion that follows on information, the leading and lagging indicators of strategic performance comprise the agenda for these quarterly meetings. The governance committee must also interface with the compensation committee of the board in terms of linking corporate objectives to the incentive compensation system.

The governance committee should also become familiar with the execution and operations activities of the enterprise through periodic field visits and meetings with management. The governance committee must have as great a familiarity with the decision-making processes of the enterprise as the audit committee has of the financial outcomes of those decisions.

Executive Management—Policy Committee   Those most senior policy-level executives who have accountability for corporate-level strategy have a frequent, probably monthly dialogue around strategic decisions and the consequences of those decisions. Those five or six most senior executives, led by the chief executive officer, will be interested in execution and operational activities as well as the implementation of the policy required to enable those activities. For example, it is not enough to approve decisions and to monitor the consequences of those decisions. It is also important that all levels of management are living the policies. The feedback and learning that are so much a part of Systems Thinking must become an integral part of the fabric of the enterprise. It is through such feedback and learning that organizations benefit from their good as well as their bad decisions. It is also important to note that feedback and learning are outside-in activities. The perspective of the policy committee must be external if the enterprise is to survive and grow.

As was the case with the governance committee of the board, executive management must spend time in the field with:

- Operating management
- Customers
- Suppliers
- Investors
- Regulators

It is only through frequent contact at the level of the organization where value is created does executive management learn what is happening. It is also through such field involvement that the share owners and stakeholders of the Extended Enterprise share in the direction of the organization. In my experience, there is no substitute for the involvement of executive management with individuals outside the corporate headquarters. This involvement provides executive management with a firsthand opportunity to listen to and observe the consequences of their decisions.

Senior Management—Executive Committee   Most organizations with which I have worked have an executive committee that is comprised of the policy-level executives described earlier as well as the next 12 to 14 leaders of business units, functions, and other activities. The executive committee is accountable for executing the strategies developed at a corporate level through those business units, functions, and activities. Executive committees meet monthly, primarily to update each other regarding the status of business plans, major programs, and projects. While the group is fairly large, and decisions generally are not made at this level, the executive committee serves an important feedback and learning purpose. If the executive committee meetings, usually chaired by the chief operating officer, are conducted in an open, collegial way, the experiences of all attendees constitute a powerful forum for learning. If the meetings foster political posturing and self-serving attitudes, the meetings do more harm than good. From a process standpoint, the CEO should use the executive committee as a training ground for the next generation of policy-level decision makers.

Operating Management—Operations Committee   The activities of the operations subsystem of the Governance Model and the System of Governance depend on clear, consistent coordination, communication, and cooperation among those who are responsible for the day-to-day running of the business. Indeed, this requirement for people to effectively and efficiently work together is the task of management that Peter Drucker introduced 50 years ago.

The operations committee is often chaired by an executive vice president to whom many of the operational and administrative functions report. In many ways this senior officer, who also sits on the execution and policy committees, is the field coach or manager of the team. It is through his or her effective coaching that the day-to-day activities are carried out and learning occurs.

The operations committee represents the first line of defense in terms of the consequences of the Extended Enterprise. An effective operations committee, through its membership of department heads and supervisors, is quick to understand and take action around the consequences of decisions or the implementation of projects that either are failing to meet or are exceeding expectations.

In many organizations, the operations committee meets for brief periods once a week. The agenda consists of those early warning signals that precede some form of operational, execution, or strategic problem or opportunity throughout the Extended Enterprise. Since the consequences of most decisions occur at different times and places from the decisions that created them, close attention to even the weakest operational signal is important. This is what I mean by the operations committee forming the first line of defense within the Extended Enterprise.

Information

The information element of the organization, management process, and information subsystem of the Governance Model is really the circulatory system of the model. Information passes throughout all of the subsystems of the model, recording statuses and sharing metrics. The metaphor of a circulatory system inside an organic organization is helpful in terms of understanding how the model sends, receives, and uses information to monitor, track, and compare results. The most important reason why, among the Big Decisions discussed earlier, a single information system is stressed is that multiple circulatory systems will transmit and receive different, often conflicting, signals. One information system is mandatory to an effective Governance Model and System of Governance. For the purposes of this discussion, one information system does not mean that all information is shared throughout the enterprise, and that there is not different information for different purposes. One information system does mean that all of the information presented within the organization is internally consistent and is generally derived from the same databases. One information system records decisions taken at all levels and traces the implications on those decisions throughout the Extended Enterprise.

For the purposes of the Governance Model, information is not all quantitative or derived from accounting systems. Information may range from memoranda regarding competitor action through the most detailed operating transaction. Information may be uncertain and anticipatory, such as future corporate objectives, or may be historical facts. Information may originate outside of the enterprise, such as trade association or governmental statistics, or from deep within the operating systems of the enterprise. Perhaps most important, information of all sorts should pass among all units of the Extended Enterprise, including:

- Customers and customers-to-be
- Suppliers
- Regulators and rating agencies
- Competitors

Finally, information must be logically defined as cause or effect, input or output, leading or lagging. The Governance Model is a decision-making framework with the results of those decisions depicted as outcomes, results, risk, and reward. The role of information within the Governance Model, therefore, is to connect those decisions with the information required to provide feedback and learning around the consequences of those decisions.

Information Framework   The Governance Model provides the framework for organizing information in the same way that it forms a framework for decision-making and management process:

- Strategy
- Execution
- Operations

At the strategy level, the Big Decisions provide the table of contents, so to speak, for the information required to track the planned outcomes of those decisions as well as a pathway for tracking the consequences of those decisions. For example, corporate objectives are established by the policy committee and reviewed and approved by the board. The board and executive management, through the objective-setting process, establish, among other outcomes, the growth and profitability targets for the enterprise. Those targets often are established year-by-year for the next four to five years as part of the strategic planning process. Those targets, in turn, become goals at the execution level and budget assumptions at the operations level. The board and other levels of decision making will track performance compared to those objectives, goals, and budget assumptions as an element of management process outlined earlier. Figure 9.1 outlines the cause and effect and feedback loop associated with this set of decisions.

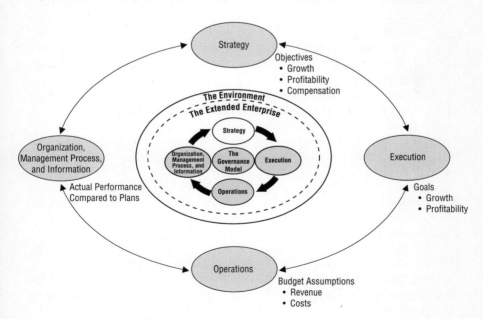

FIGURE 9.1   Example of Financial Decisions

Strategic objectives drive execution goals. If, for some reason, the strategic objectives may not be aligned with the execution goals or do not translate into the next year's budget assumptions, the objectives, goals, and budget assumptions are worked through the various management processes until such congruence is achieved. The board and the various management organizations monitor actual performance compared to agreed-upon plans and take corrective action as necessary.

Information Framework and Corporate Culture   The Governance Model and the System of Governance depend almost entirely on the information framework to permit feedback and learning to take place. Information of all types—qualitative and quantitative, strategic and operational—flows through the Governance Model and provides circulation to the System of Governance. It is for this reason that one information system is a Big Decision.

Over time, information becomes baked into the cultural fabric of the Extended Enterprise. Objective, fact-based dialogue, using information as an agenda becomes the means of achieving communication, coordination, and cooperation—the role of management. Without a reliable, trusted system of information, behavior becomes power-based and political. Whatever information is used for decision making becomes self-serving and biased.

I interviewed Marvin Rich, executive vice president of HealthNet, a Woodland Hills, California—based managed health care company with $10 billion in annual revenue. I have known Marv since my days at WellPoint, where he developed the executive information system that is credited with helping to facilitate the fact-based decision-making culture within that enterprise.

A significant amount of space in this section on information is devoted to the interview with Marv because of all of the executives I have known, he has done the most effective job in facilitating organizational change through the implementation of management information systems. As Marv says, "Change comes through the power of information and fact-based decision making."

Marv had considerable experience prior to WellPoint as an information systems specialist and later as chief financial officer of a number of organizations. Following WellPoint, Marv implemented his information strategy at Kmart and facilitated what turned out to be a temporary turnaround at that organization. After Kmart, Marv moved on to Oxford Health, where he helped Dr. Payson with the remarkable turnaround in that now successful enterprise (discussed in Chapter 3). Marv spent some time helping to rationalize the WebMD organization before moving on to HealthNet, where he has also made a real difference.

During our discussion, I asked Marv to outline his first principles for successful organizational change through information:

■ Prioritize the drivers of change required into the top five or six key initiatives together with the same number of metrics that may be used to track progress. Such prioritization places a focus on the sequence in which the operating systems of the enterprise must be fixed. For example, an obvious driver in the managed care industry, of course, is the cost of care, which, in turn, places a primary emphasis on an effective claims processing system.

■ Link the information requirement to the source operating system, which, in turn, focuses attention on that system and facilitates its improvement or replacement.

■ "Everybody gets to see the data." The peer pressure for improvement in both the operating results and the underlying system dramatically shortcuts the time to correct both issues.

■ "Take advantage of the well-known Hawthorn Effect," which in today's language translates into the observer and the observed. That is, the fact that those responsible for overseeing the results of operations (the observers) are part of the same information system and management process as those who must fix the operation (the observed) causes feedback and learning to occur at an accelerated pace. Marvin's point here is that management process and information drive change, a point I try to make using Systems Thinking as a means of changing the way people look at the world.

■ "Trends are your friend." The point here is that business graphics and the ability to visualize relative performance set up a dialogue that may be more persuasive than merely looking at columns of numbers.

■ "You can't bring your own data." The only way the operating systems get cleaned up and the appropriate metrics become reliable is for the data to be all there is for senior and operating management to review and upon which to take action. I saw this phenomenon work very effectively at WellPoint.

Marv's "first principles" are at once very intuitive and very difficult to put in place. As he related to me, it requires a risk taker such as himself and a CEO who gets it, such as Leonard Schaeffer at WellPoint, Dr. Payson at Oxford, and Jay Gellert at HealthNet. With such support, resource allocation decisions are much clearer. Reliable tracking of the results of such decisions at all levels of the enterprise really provides the learning and feedback necessary for the improvement in future decisions to take place.

I am very grateful to Marvin Rich for his willingness to share his first-hand experience with me. His comments provide an excellent testimonial to the role of management process and information regarding the issues of governance and risk. In fact, at the end of our interview Marv remarked, "You don't have to try to manage the results people are supposed to achieve if you can help them to better manage their decisions."

Information Framework and Organizational Learning   The major characteristic of Systems Thinking is that of feedback and learning. The Governance Model requires feedback and learning to take place in order to anticipate, understand, and take action around the consequences of choices and decisions. Intended and unintended consequences are either magnified (i.e., rewards) or minimized (i.e., risks) as a direct result of feedback and learning. Individuals at all levels become better at their jobs and are better teachers if they have consistent and clear information as a basis for dialogue with their colleagues.

Again using WellPoint as an example, meetings at all levels are conducted using what they call their Business Information System as the agenda. One base of facts is available and displayed on a screen. Few, if any, paper reports are needed. Questions are surfaced, discussed, and, if necessary, "drill-downs" through the hierarchy of information provide additional facts. The dialogue that takes place is open and clear. Everyone is learning all the time. Meetings are generally work sessions, not presentations. The decisions that emerge from such meetings are thoughtful and are based on input from all participants. The results of decisions are much better in terms of anticipation and understanding of intended and unintended consequences. The continued success of the enterprise is a direct result of information-based decision making.

A Note of Caution   Earlier, in the Big Decisions section of this chapter, I noted four decisions that apply to the organization, management process, and information framework:

- One information system for the Extended Enterprise.
- Keep it simple.
- Precision is not required.
- Fast-track implementation.

While all of the Big Decisions apply to all three issues raised in this chapter, those decisions must be applied most rigorously in the information framework. I have already discussed the requirement for one system.

The other three are equally important. "Keep it simple" means the selection of few metrics as leading and lagging indicators. Nothing will slow down implementation more than too much data. Keep it simple means working backward from the decisions taken at each level, identifying the one or two measures of performance for that level, and then identifying the drivers or so-called leading indicators that link cause and effect. For example, one business unit serving one market segment simply cannot manage more than five or six drivers. All of the metrics for a fairly large, $1 billion insurance company should not exceed 20. Keep it simple also means top-down. Attempting to implement a system of information by first trying to identify and assemble all of the pieces does not work. By the time all of the pieces were assembled, if ever, and systematically built from the ground up, the enterprise and the external environment would have changed so much as to make the effort obsolete long before it could possible be completed.

"Precision is not required" means, in addition to being top-down in its orientation, information must be reliable, but not so focused on ultra levels of precision that the compilation process exceeds the value of the information. This point does not mean that accounting records—the past—need not be accurately recorded and within professional standards. This point means that the focus of the most valuable information is the future. The events haven't occurred yet, or if they have occurred, such as customer service or employee attitudes, they do not flow through the accounting records, anyway. The decisions that will be made at each level of the Governance Model—essentially decisions regarding the future—do not require accounting-level precision regarding the past to be effective decisions.

"Fast-track implementation" means getting something up and running immediately while the system is required and the information useful. As pointed out earlier, a bottom-up implementation does not work. Nor does a multiyear implementation work. This does not mean that an effective information framework won't take years to implement. It will. What it does mean is that the system must be implemented, at least in a rudimentary way, for feedback and learning to take place.

The most effective blocking mechanism or antichange behavior I have encountered over the years has been around the subject of information. Freely available, fact-based information changes the balance of power in an organization. Multiple systems, complexity, precision, and long-term implementation schedules are very effective in resisting change of any nature in any enterprise.

CONCLUSION

The successful implementation of the organization, management process, and information subsystems of the Governance Model and the System of Governance is a prerequisite for the Systems Thinking approach to work.

Governance (the decision-making processes) and risk (the consequences of those decisions) work only when there is structure to hold them together. The subsystems of strategy, execution, and operations are ineffective if taken separately. They become a whole when they are connected. And they are connected through:

- Organization—who
- Management process—how
- Information framework—what

All three must be present and working together.

This chapter concludes the discussion of the Governance Model and the System of Governance. These four chapters have discussed what must be done around the subject of governance and risk and why they must be discussed together. The following chapters will introduce other players in the Extended Enterprise and the process by which the Governance Model and the System of Governance are implemented.

Implementing the Perspective

Making It Happen

INTRODUCTION

Implementation of the Governance Model and the System of Governance involves choices and decisions, just as the strategy, execution, and operations subsystems of the Governance Model require decisions to be made. In this instance we are talking about the implementation of the Governance Model itself as opposed to decisions around direction, execution, and operations of the enterprise. In other words, the Governance Model is a framework for decision making at all levels of the enterprise. The framework is static. It has not been brought to life. The implementation of the Governance Model is a process whereby the Governance Model comes to life. The implementation process converts the static model into a dynamic, living way of anticipating, understanding, and taking action around the choices available and the outcomes or consequences of decisions made from among those choices.

In a way, this chapter is about the management of change, but it doesn't end there. There has been an enormous amount of material generated around the subject of change and the management of change. Each author has his or her own model of what works. Probably all of the models work—in the contexts in which those models were developed. In other situations, the same change model may be singularly ineffective. In the context of governance and risk, how should the board and executive management consider the implementation of the Governance Model?

I think the first question to be asked and answered is, "How do we get the attention of the board and executive management?" If the change in perception that we highlight in Chapter 2 is what it takes to consider a different way of looking at the world, how do we ignite that change in perception? How does the process begin? As usual, the answer probably rests with an individual or visionary who sees both the problem and its solution, and has the personal courage to act.

CREATING THE SPARK

As I have examined change in a variety of settings—political, social, organizational, or even process or technological—the common theme always seems to be an enlightened individual. Organizations don't make change; a few people make change.

Just as an aside, when I speak of creating the spark that ignites the change process, I am not referring to personal charisma. I am speaking of bright, insightful leaders who by dint of their own history and credibility earn the right to speak. Such leaders may or may not have what we may call charisma. What they all have in common is that intangible, elusive, impossible-to-define trait I have come to call "star quality."

The leader with my so-called star quality may be a director or perhaps a trusted outside advisor. The leader may be a member of executive management who tends to see the world differently than his or her colleagues. The leader must not only be personally capable of seeing the world differently; he or she must also be capable, usually as a teacher, to stimulate others to see the world differently as well. Lastly, the leader must have something to teach. In the context of this book, the leader must first embrace and then convince others on the merits of the Governance Model.

To the board member, CEO, or member of executive management who reads this, perhaps you are the leader who creates the spark. Or, perhaps, you and one of your colleagues may collaborate to create the pathway to change. Whoever you are or however you approach the talk of change, remember it takes a spark to ignite the force for change.

WHY IS CHANGE SO DIFFICULT?

Organizations don't make change; people make change. Mature people don't change much, and mature organizations don't change much. The behavior, therefore, of mature people, hence mature organizations, is rewarded by what made them successful in the first place. In large organizations, success is most often achieved by those who play by the rules. As we saw earlier, rule-based negative feedback loops create stability and avoid chaos. Stable, risk-averse behavior is rewarded, and such behavior becomes the norm in mature organizations. Rocking the boat is not a valued behavior. Conversely, change in emerging organizations is relatively easy. There is little to be changed. Emerging organizations that are successful generally make it because they are willing to challenge the status quo of mature organizations. Interestingly, it doesn't take long for emerging organizations to adopt the change-resistant behavior of their more mature counterparts.

WHAT KINDS OF CHANGE ARE REQUIRED?

The implementation of the Governance Model and the System of Governance that have been the subject of this book requires a change in perception and thinking from a piecemeal, transaction, or silo approach to what has been constantly referred to as Systems Thinking. This is a different kind of change in most organizations. This is not strategic, execution, or operational change. This is not about a new business model, a new set of business processes, or a new operations methodology. This change is about a change in how decisions are made and how feedback and learning take place.

Individual organizational situations seem to dictate the kind of change required for the implementation of the Governance Model and the System of Governance. I think that there are two fundamental models of change:

1. Transitional change
2. Transformational change

I will introduce each type of change in the context of the organizational situation and then elaborate in greater depth the strategy each type of organization may employ in the implementation of such change.

Transitional Change Strategy

In a few settings, the change in decision-making processes—that is, a change to the Governance Model—is much more of a transitional change. Many boards and executive managements apply cause and effect, feedback and learning almost intuitively to nearly all of their decision making. Recall in Chapters 3 and 9 my reference to an acquisition that was not made after careful due diligence revealed that the fundamental culture of the business would change. That decision was a direct result of the organization's ability to examine the potential consequences or outcomes of its decisions. While the organization in question would not characterize the decision-making process as a reflection of Systems Thinking, the approach in fact employed the basic concepts of Systems Thinking. Implementation of the Governance Model in those organizations that make relatively few Big Decisions and are careful in their decision-making processes will be a rather straightforward process. Indeed, in my discussions with organizations that employ feedback and learning in their decision making, the transition to the proposed Governance Model becomes a natural evolution and is quickly embraced. In a way, the Governance Model provides the framework that explains what they have, in large measure, been doing all along. Very little change in perception is required.

Transitional change to the Governance Model and the System of Governance may apply to the 10 to 15 percent of organizations that embrace good decision-making and governance practices anyway. The Governance Model will help them improve what are already best practices and provide a framework for leadership and management development. Well-run enterprises are always looking for ways to improve.

Transformational Change Strategy

In most settings, the change to the proposed Governance Model will be transformational. That is, the basic form of the decision making must be changed. Those organizations I characterized as fragmented in Chapter 2 will face fundamental change in all manner of decision making if they are to employ Systems Thinking and implement the Governance Model. Simply stated, in the vast majority of cases, how enterprises approach their Big Decisions will have to change.

Transformational change, as I indicated earlier, requires a change in perspective at an individual level. Organizations don't change perspective. Generally speaking, it is individuals from outside the enterprise that bring the change in perspective. Seldom are the voices for change heard from within the organization.

Most often new voices arrive as a result of the "burning platform" or major upheaval brought about by:

- Bankruptcy.
- Poorly managed crisis.
- Scandal, defalcation, or major regulatory issues.
- Escalation of a seemingly small event into a catastrophe.
- Acquisition or merger.
- Loss of board confidence in the CEO.

The replacement of the board in some cases, and the CEO in many cases, introduces the opportunity for the transformation. The question most often asked is, "Transformation to what?" In many if not most instances, the change from one situation to another, or from the old voices to the new voices, does not generate much change at all. This is simply because the worldview of most of us does not change regardless of our circumstances. We bring our "baggage" along with us wherever we go. It is only when we are able to break the cycle of historical patterns of behavior and decision making does the opportunity for transformational change take place. This is where the voice of the leader—one who sees the world differently—begins to be heard. This is where a framework such as the

Governance Model is available to answer the question, "Transformation to what?"

Bringing It All Together

Transitional or evolutionary change is available to those relatively few organizations that have a historical record of survival and growth. The leaders and managers of those organizations have already demonstrated that they can establish a fit between the Extended Enterprise and its environment. They intuitively understand the implications of cause and effect, feedback and learning. Implementation of the Governance Model is a natural extension of their current perspective.

Transformation or revolutionary change is required for those organizations whose survival and growth has been, and is likely to continue to be, at risk. These organizations, for whatever reasons, have failed to establish a fit between the Extended Enterprise and its environment. Transformational change is required for the implementation of the Governance Model and the System of Governance.

Finally, transformational change is required for those organizations that would have been successful except for a basic failure of values. I brought forward the issue of Tone at the Top very early in this book. Such failure has brought on spectacular disasters from Ivan Boesky and Michael Milken to Kenneth Lay and Dennis Kozlowski. In these situations, survival and growth are totally dependent on a transformation not only of the Tone at the Top, but of the entire process of governance, from the boardroom to the day-to-day transaction-processing activities. The Governance Model and the System of Governance may provide frameworks for decision making and organization, but they cannot provide values. Values may only come from doing the right thing, not just what is legal.

PHASES OF IMPLEMENTATION

The remainder of this chapter will deal with strategies that in my experience have resulted in successful use of the Governance Model and the System of Governance. The following sections deal with the three phases of implementation, including:

- Phase I (Diagnostic)—determination of the changes required in the decision-making processes.
- Phase II (Prescriptive)—process designed to implement the specifics of the Governance Model.

■ Phase III (Monitoring)—continuous mapping and tracking of the implementation process.

PRECONDITIONS FOR SUCCESSFUL CHANGE

The following preconditions for successful implementation are incorporated in the three phases of implementation regardless of whether the proposed change is transitional or transformational:

1. A *reason* for making a change to a different framework for decision making.
2. A *clear picture* of the Governance Model when fully in place.
3. A *process* for making the change to the Governance Model.

Back to the Present

I like to see the "Back to the Present" model in Figure 10.1 as a way of thinking about the three preconditions. I start out with at least a provisional understanding and acceptance that some form of change is required, and then move toward establishing a clear picture of the future, followed by how we may get to that future state. By simultaneously accepting the fact that change is necessary, together with a shared framework of the future, as well as a view of the journey to that future, individuals at the board and executive management levels may internalize the preconditions for change. The "Back to the Present" model works well because people may see themselves in that future. There is a there there, to paraphrase Gertrude Stein. Individual and collective understanding and acceptance are gained along with the commitment to take the trip.

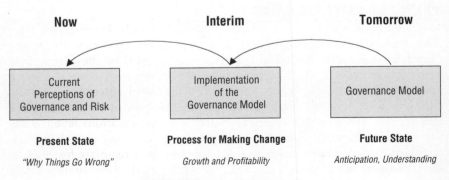

FIGURE 10.1 Back to the Present

The logic of this book follows the "Back to the Present" model. First, I tried to build a case for a different perspective—Systems Thinking; then I established the future state—the Governance Model; and now I am discussing the process for making change. I hope that it helps in your approach to your own situation.

TRANSITIONAL CHANGE STRATEGY

As pointed out earlier, the top performers in any industry or sector are characterized as being well led and managed. Leadership and management are what propels them to the top, and in a few instances keeps them there, for at least a generation or two. Effective leaders and managers are often intuitive decision makers, but in my experience, they all have adapted to one degree or another decision-making processes that work for them. Really effective leaders have their decision-making processes so well established that they can teach them and have such processes replicated throughout the enterprise. Such leaders are actually continuously guiding their organizations from one state to another as they adapt to their environment and anticipate the needs, wants, and expectations of their customers. These organizations survive and grow in good and bad economic times.

The transition to the Governance Model and the System of Governance for successful enterprises is an evolutionary means to achieving continuous improvement, in this instance around governance and risk. Successful organizations understand and embrace change, and the implementation of the Governance Model is but another milestone in the journey of continuous improvement.

Phase I (Diagnostic)—Determination of the Changes Required in the Decision-Making Processes

Successful organizations are characterized not only by effective decision making—governance; they intuitively understand that they must improve their processes. The question is, what will be the form of the new processes?

The Phase I (Diagnostic) activity for successful enterprises uses the Governance Model as a framework for the analysis of current decision-making processes at the strategic, execution, and operations levels of the Extended Enterprise. The organization, management process, and information subsystem of the Governance Model serves as a template for examining how well the System of Governance is holding the Governance Model together as a system.

To be more specific, the Big Decisions that are outlined in each of the chapters that describe the Governance Model also serve as useful examples of decision making at each level of the Extended Enterprise.

Using the framework and tools illustrated throughout this book, the Phase I (Diagnostic) activity serves to define the current state of governance throughout the enterprise, from the board to transaction processing. The diagnostic process serves to establish a gap between the current practices or state of decision making and the future state—the Governance Model.

The gap analysis establishes exactly what needs to be done throughout the Extended Enterprise to achieve the transition to the Governance Model and the System of Governance. For example, at the strategy level, the diagnostic activity examines the Big Decisions that were made or not made from among the choices available to the board and executive management. The diagnostic also identifies the tools—such as scenario planning, real options theory, or decision tree analysis—to determine how such decisions were made. Most importantly, the diagnostic examines the extent to which the outcomes—risks and rewards—of such decisions are tracked throughout the Extended Enterprise and the degree to which feedback and learning take place.

The Phase I (Diagnostic) activity is not what is commonly referred to as a risk assessment study. Remember, in our worldview of Systems Thinking, cause and effect, feedback and learning, risk and reward are outcomes or results of choices available and decisions made or not made from among those choices. Our perspective or assessment, which we call diagnosis, focuses on decisions and how decisions were taken. Certainly some risks or outcomes are known and are nearly always present in most organizations. Our concern is not to try to anticipate every risk or reward that could occur, but first to examine the decision-making process; then to assess the decisions; and finally to anticipate, understand, and, if appropriate, take action around the outcomes—risks and rewards—of those decisions. It is also appropriate here to reemphasize that the Governance Model is a dynamic, real-time examination of decision making, while a risk assessment is a static view of those risks that may be visualized at a point in time.

Who Performs the Phase I Diagnostic Work?   In mature, stable, successful enterprises, organizational structures and management processes for considering risk probably are already in place. In some instances, there is a chief risk officer (CRO) who is charged with the responsibility for enterprise-wide risk management. In other situations, the chief financial officer (CFO) or legal counsel may take the leadership of a change initiative. Finally, there may be a trusted outside advisor who serves as a catalyst or force for change to bring together the appropriate resources from throughout the Extended Enterprise to undertake the diagnostic activity. In all situations, there is the champion or enlightened individual I spoke of earlier in this chapter. That enlightened individual may not take a leadership role in the process, but he or she definitely provides the spark to ignite the process.

Regardless of who takes the lead, the approach should be top-down and broad enough in scope to cover the accountability for the Big Decisions across all levels of the Extended Enterprise. Speaking of the Extended Enterprise, the scope of the diagnostic should be broad enough to anticipate and understand the consequences of the decisions made among at least the major constituents of the Extended Enterprise as described in Chapter 4. As stated earlier, "No ship sails on its own bottom." We are all connected in one way or another.

The diagnostic team should consist not only of subject-matter experts (i.e., strategy, finance, technology, human resources, marketing, and operations), but also individuals who have a good grasp of Systems Thinking. This different perspective is absolutely essential to the use of the Governance Model as a framework or tool for diagnosing the current state of enterprise-wide decision making.

How Long Should the Phase I Diagnostic Take to Complete?   In my experience, working with medium-size—$500 million to $5 billion in revenue—organizations or business units of similar size in larger corporations, a 60- to 90-day time frame should be enough. Diagnostic activities that take longer usually lose momentum and get lost in the details. Remember, this is a top-down process. The diagnostic activities should be thought of as important, intense, and thorough. The effort in the medium-size enterprise usually consists of no more than a dozen subject-matter experts deployed on as nearly a full-time basis as possible for a time frame short enough to get the job done with the quality required to anticipate and understand how the Big Decisions are made throughout the Extended Enterprise.

What Are the End Products of the Phase I Diagnostic?   As indicated earlier, the Governance Model and the Big Decisions establish the framework for analysis. Therefore, the table of contents of Phase I (Diagnostic) should pretty closely follow that framework. By establishing the table of contents in advance of the starting of the diagnostic activity, each member of the team gains a visual understanding of what is expected. The table of contents serves three other uses as well:

1. A framework for establishing a plan for the project.
2. An outline or discussion guide for communicating results.
3. An introduction to what must be done in Phase II (Prescriptive) to close the gap between the current and future states of decision making within the Extended Enterprise.

Who Is the Audience for the Phase I Diagnostic?   In a word, everyone! What must be done to transition the decision-making processes from where we are to where we wish to be is everyone's business. In a world of cause and effect, feedback and learning, decisions made throughout the Extended Enterprise have outcomes and consequences that surface in different places and at different times. As a result, everyone has a stake in improving the decision-making processes throughout the Extended Enterprise. The board of directors, who has primary accountability for at least the strategic decisions and their consequences, clearly needs to be involved in changes to the governance processes. Executive, senior, and operating management all have a vested interest, accountability, and responsibility for the feedback and learning that must take place in order for the Governance Model to be effective.

Phase II (Prescriptive)—A Process Designed to Implement the Specifics of the Governance Model

Successful organizations have learned how to implement new processes. If this sounds like a self-evident statement, it probably is. However, when one considers how few management processes are really implemented in the manner in which they were designed, the statement may not be as obvious as it seems. Successful organizations really learn how to make change. Middle-of-the-road organizations tend to be carried along by inertia.

As stated earlier in this chapter, change occurs when there is a demonstrated reason to change and a process by which the change itself is managed. Phase I (Diagnostic) provided the rationale for continued improvement, the gap analysis. Phase I also provided the view of the future, the Governance Model. Phase II then provides the methodology for closing the gap and achieving the future state.

Once the diagnostic team has completed its work, received board and executive management approval, and communicated the future state to the rest of the Extended Enterprise, an activity time line is established for the coming year. Recall that one of the end products of Phase I was a definition of what must be done to close the gap between the current and the future state. The definition of what is established using the Governance Model as the framework:

- Strategy
- Execution
- Operations
- Organization, management process, and information

Plan to Plan   The proposed activity time line is what I call a "Plan to Plan," shown in Figure 10.2. The Governance Model is actually implemented by performing the activities that are called out in the "Management" section of each chapter describing the Governance Model.

- Roles and responsibilities
- Processes/activities

Those sections are designed to identify, for each subsystem of the Governance Model, who is responsible for what. The "Plan to Plan" time line shown in Figure 10.2 is established and approved well in advance of the annual planning cycle of the enterprise. It is through the execution of the plan that the Governance Model and the System of Governance are implemented. As described in the earlier chapters, strategy, execution, and operations plans are carried out by those who have direct accountability and responsibility for achieving those plans.

In summary, the Governance Model and the System of Governance are implemented by carrying out the management activities outlined within the model themselves. This is an exercise that creates both form and substance in one Plan to Plan. The Governance Model is bootstrapped by its own processes. It is through this learning-by-doing process that not only is the Governance Model implemented, but the feedback and learning required to gain true understanding and acceptance take place. To flesh out the Plan to Plan in greater depth, it may be useful at this point to read through Chapters 7 to 10 once again.

Phase III (Monitoring)—The Continuous Mapping and Tracking of the Implementation Process

As stated earlier, the implementation of even transformational change within successful organizations requires constant attention. Successful enterprises simply manage change better than their less successful counterparts.

What Do Successful Companies Do?   It has been my experience that the policy-level executives not only commit to the principles of continuous improvement, they visibly follow up and monitor, in this case, the Plan to Plan. The governance, policy, executive, and operations committees, led by the CEO and the champion or sponsor of the intended change, constantly follow up, ask questions, and provide the energy and guidance to keep the process on track. I cannot overemphasize the importance of continuous mapping and tracking of the implementation process. Change, even change within a successful enterprise, won't happen without such attention.

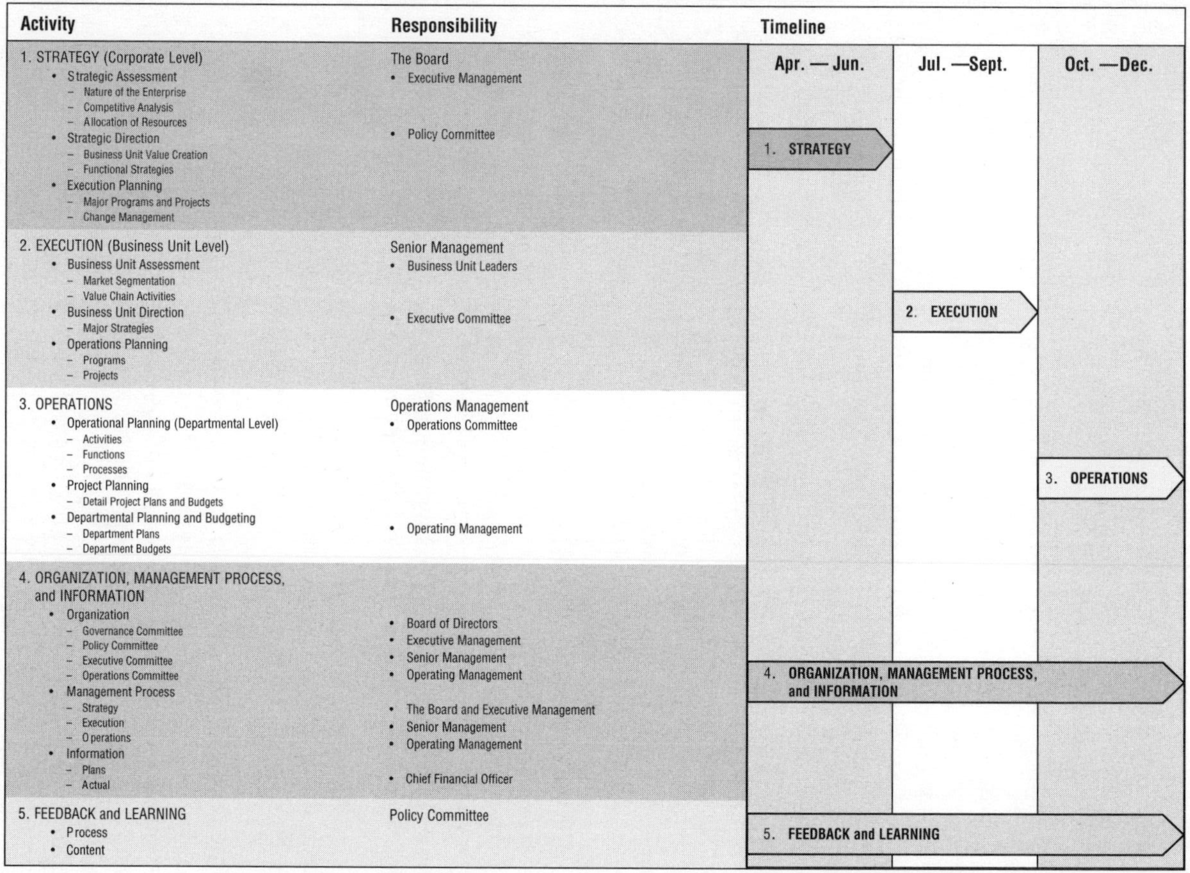

Activity	Responsibility	Timeline		
		Apr. — Jun.	Jul. —Sept.	Oct. —Dec.

1. STRATEGY (Corporate Level)
• Strategic Assessment
  – Nature of the Enterprise
  – Competitive Analysis
  – Allocation of Resources
• Strategic Direction
  – Business Unit Value Creation
  – Functional Strategies
• Execution Planning
  – Major Programs and Projects
  – Change Management
	The Board
	• Executive Management
	
	• Policy Committee
		1. STRATEGY		

2. EXECUTION (Business Unit Level)
• Business Unit Assessment
  – Market Segmentation
  – Value Chain Activities
• Business Unit Direction
  – Major Strategies
• Operations Planning
  – Programs
  – Projects
	Senior Management
	• Business Unit Leaders
	
	• Executive Committee
			2. EXECUTION	

3. OPERATIONS
• Operational Planning (Departmental Level)
  – Activities
  – Functions
  – Processes
• Project Planning
  – Detail Project Plans and Budgets
• Departmental Planning and Budgeting
  – Department Plans
  – Department Budgets
	Operations Management
	• Operations Committee
	
	• Operating Management
				3. OPERATIONS

4. ORGANIZATION, MANAGEMENT PROCESS, and INFORMATION
• Organization
  – Governance Committee
  – Policy Committee
  – Executive Committee
  – Operations Committee
• Management Process
  – Strategy
  – Execution
  – Operations
• Information
  – Plans
  – Actual
	• Board of Directors
	• Executive Management
	• Senior Management
	• Operating Management
	
	• The Board and Executive Management
	• Senior Management
	• Operating Management
	• Chief Financial Officer
		4. ORGANIZATION, MANAGEMENT PROCESS, and INFORMATION		

5. FEEDBACK and LEARNING • Process • Content	Policy Committee	5. FEEDBACK and LEARNING		

FIGURE 10.2 The Plan to Plan—Implementation of the Governance Model

The Plan to Plan provides the framework for the activities, tasks, roles, responsibilities, and end products to be mapped and tracked. The Plan to Plan contains many interdependencies and requirements for certain activities to be completed before others are undertaken. If such relationships between activities are not constantly monitored and corrective action is not taken, the entire implement effort is at risk.

Finally, at the completion of the first year of the Governance Model implementation process, I have found it useful to follow up and assess the process. I have asked each member of the organization to fill out the questionnaire and e-mail it to me with the commitment on my part to keep such replies confidential. Upon receiving the feedback, I first cut off the e-mail header that contains the respondent's name, then sort all of the responses by question. As I review all of the responses to each question, I create a summary for feedback and learning purposes. Once the summary has been edited, I have found it useful to then distribute it to the participants in advance of a workshop designed to work through the strengths and weaknesses of the implementation process. The dialogue generated at the workshop is then used to modify the Plan to Plan for the following year. Once again, I am using the feedback and learning principles of Systems Thinking to provide continuous improvement.

Bringing Transitional Change to a Close

In some ways, this section on implementation makes me feel as though I am "preaching to the converted." Successful organizations rigorously adhere to the principles of continuous improvement every day. In addressing those organizations that already implement change well, I am only trying to provide a framework for a best practice designed to enhance their governance processes. Hopefully, such organizations may get even better or reach a higher plateau as a result of the successful implementation of the Governance Model.

For those enterprises that are middle-of-the-road, average organizations, this section on best practices of successful companies may provide a glimpse of how they may proceed with transitional change once they have launched themselves on the track of transformational change. The next section of this chapter is designed to describe that level of change.

TRANSFORMATIONAL CHANGE STRATEGY

As I introduce the topic of transformational change, I will avoid repeating those passages and exhibits that are common to both types of change. This section will deal with the differences between transitional and transformational change.

I have alluded to the point on a number of occasions, that most improvements in most organizations are temporary. Successful organizations come and go as new competitors with new ideas and innovative processes come on the scene. Other organizations, usually larger, stable household names, are carried forward until they topple as a result of their own weight. Those organizations may be carried forward by inertia. The reality is, perhaps for a generation a two, such organizations reside right in the middle of the pack. They are surviving but not growing. Both survival and growth are necessary to provide share owner value and to serve all of their stakeholders.

Transformational change is the required approach when:

■ A formerly successful organization falls behind and is no longer growing.
■ A large, mature organization is not growing and survival is at stake.
■ A merger or acquisition is pending.
■ Some form of scandal is unearthed.
■ There is a change in leadership.

Without going into each one of these triggers of change, it is obviously important to understand which event or combination of events is at the root of the survival and growth issue. Reviewing the phases of implementation of the Governance Model will help to underscore what problem we are trying to solve.

Phase I (Diagnostic)—Determination of the Changes Required in the Decision-Making Processes

This phase, rather than focusing on continuous improvement and gap analysis, will recognize the reality that most if not all of the governance and decision-making processes must be replaced. It is the decisions and decision-making processes that, over the long run, caused the crises of survival and growth. Diagnostic activity associated with transformational change must clearly conclude that the future state of governance and decision making will take the form of the Governance Model, at least for the purpose of this book.

Transformational change is a top-down process, nearly always involving a new leader. It is the new leader who establishes the Governance Model as the future state of the enterprise. I have worked in any number of turnaround situations, and it is invariably the captain of the ship who decides both the destination and the course to be steered. It is my hope and expectation that this book may help the new leader with a model of the future as well as a process for achieving that future.

When we apply Systems Thinking and the concepts of cause and effect, feedback and learning to the task of Phase I (Diagnostic), it is critical that the choice of decision-making process not create more problems than solutions. If the new leader is to achieve longevity in his or her position, the selection of a framework and process for implementation becomes his or her first Big Decision. For example, the CEO who feels that he or she must call all the shots or dominate the agenda will not survive. The new leader, even if that leader is an experienced turnaround artist (as they often like to be characterized), cannot possibly grasp the range of outcomes of their decisions—their risks.

For those leaders who do embrace the Governance Model as the preferred framework for decision making, the four subsystems of the model are still the appropriate implementation activities. The time frames for implementation may be shortened; the use of tools and methodologies may be either simplified or dealt with at a high level; and the number of participants in the process may be reduced.

Phase I (Diagnostic), while using the Governance Model as a framework for analysis, will develop a short list of Big Decisions, the outcomes of which will determine the future of the enterprise.

For example, the Big Decisions of strategy may include:

- A much simplified and streamlined business model.
- Allocation of scarce resources into the two to three highest-top priority projects.

The Big Decisions of execution may include:

- The naming of two or three key business unit leaders who will rigorously perform the necessary market segmentation.
- Value chain analyses.

The Big Decisions of operations may include:

- Increased emphasis on controls, particularly cash.
- Possible outsourcing of high-cost activities.

The Big Decisions of organization, management process, and information may include:

- Establishment of organizations to oversee governance processes, from the board through operations.
- A top-down set of metrics necessary to monitor key activities.

Big Decisions that emerge from Phase I (Diagnostic) should be rigorously examined as to outcomes and consequences. All too often, decisions taken in the emotion and haste of a turnaround result in risks that are greater than the original problems facing the enterprise.

Who Performs the Phase I Diagnostic Work? In my experience, the primary role of the new leader is the establishment of the future vision of the firm and the process or direction for achieving that new state. If the new leader doesn't see his or her role in establishing the new framework for governance and decision making, the new leader is probably the wrong leader. The new leader will require help—arms and legs. This is most likely an area where temporary consulting help is required. There simply isn't enough time in most turnaround situations to recruit or develop the people with the experience and skills necessary to put an entirely new system of governance in place. The new leader, however, should be the one who determines the framework for governance and the process by which that framework is implemented. I have experienced a number of situations in which the consultant or temporary management assistance people bring their own baggage or preconceived opinions of what must be done. This is not to say that consulting advice and counsel are not important. Of course they are. My point is that establishing the direction and course is the job of the new leader. Everyone else is there to help.

How Long Should the Phase I Diagnostic Take to Complete? I think that the sense of urgency for implementing the transformation strategy is best communicated to the entire enterprise by setting aggressive dates for completion of all of the phases. Certainly, Phase I (Diagnostic) should be completed and the process for implementing recommended changes undertaken within a 30- to 60-day period. It is by moving quickly and visibly demonstrating an acute sense of urgency that the entire organization comes to realize that this transformation project is not just business as usual.

What Are the End Products of the Phase I Diagnostic? As was the case with the transition strategy, the Governance Model and Big Decisions establish the table of contents for the work to be done. The table of contents sets expectations and provides a repository for all of the analysis and recommendations around what must be done. The table of contents keeps everyone on track and allows the project to be planned and managed.

Who Is the Audience for the Phase I Diagnostic? Again, the answer is everyone. It is only through the involvement of everyone from the board to operating management does the strategy for change become effective. In the world of Systems Thinking, the entire Extended Enterprise is connected and needs to be included not only in terms of the Governance Model, but in terms of the outcomes that may result from the Big Decisions. Everyone in the Extended Enterprise has a stake in the outcomes of more effective decision making—the outcomes of survival and growth.

Phase II (Prescriptive)—A Process Designed to Implement the Specifics of the Governance Model

As was the case with the transitional change strategy, the approach to implementing transformational change is accomplished by carrying out the management activities outlined within the model itself. We use the "Management" section of each chapter of the Governance Model to perform the activities called for in each subsystem of the model.

The Plan to Plan, which also forms the table of contents for the transformational strategy, lays out an accelerated schedule for completion. The time frames required to insert content into all four subsystems of the Governance Model should be abbreviated. I often use the phrase "the first 100 days" to illustrate that not only does the new broom sweep clean, but that by placing a seemingly impossible completion date on the process, only important actions are forced to be completed by a time certain. "The first 100 days" becomes the rallying cry for change with the additional message that perhaps the actions that are not prioritized for completion within the allotted time should not be undertaken at all. Another characteristic of the transformational strategy is that the work of implementing both the form and substance of the Governance Model be started immediately. It is not appropriate to justify inaction and to further reinforce the attitude of business as usual by waiting until the start of the regular planning cycle.

Finally, I believe that the transformational strategy should be carried out in terms of implementation by the members of the board, executive management, senior management, and operating management depending on the level of the Governance Model subsystem. It is entirely appropriate to seek professional help in the form of consultants or project specialists of one kind or another. However, if the consequences of decisions are to be played out and if feedback and learning are to take place across the Extended Enterprise, those who will live with the results of the process should lead the process. This is a time for both experience and learning. The tasks placed before the board and other levels of management will both take advantage of knowledge and experience throughout the enterprise and provide for important learning to occur. The System of Governance is a behavioral model and serves to hold together the Governance Model only to the extent that those who develop and implement the model operate the model on a continuous basis.

Phase III (Monitoring)—The Continuous Mapping and Tracking of the Implementation Process

The installation of the Governance Model and the System of Governance is a full-time job. There is no more important work to be done during the three to four months required to work through the diagnostic and prescriptive phases. I cannot overemphasize the point! Operations will go on; customers will be served; momentum and inertia will carry the enterprise forward just as they always have, at least for a while.

What is critical at this point in the transformation process is to get the Governance Model and the System of Governance Model installed and operating. The Big Decision of transformation will lead to much better outcomes with fewer unintended consequences if the framework and processes for decision making are right.

The monitoring and tracking of the transformation process is the work of the entire enterprise with the board and executive management monitoring and tracking the implementation of the strategy subsystem, senior management overseeing the execution subsystem, and operating management working with the operations subsystem.

In my experience, the governance committee of the board, the CEO, and the CFO take overall responsibility for the top-down implementation of the organization, management process, and information subsystem of the Governance Model at this point in the implementation of the transformation strategy. The Big Decisions around the organization, management process, and information subsystem as described in Chapter 9 are recalled:

- One information system for the Extended Enterprise.
- Keep it simple.
- Precision is not required.
- Fast-track implementation.

These points bear repeating along with the imperative that implementation be a top-down effort. Transformation of all sorts is accomplished only by establishing the organization, processes, and information as a first priority of the board and executive management. Delegating this most important change initiative to a bottom-up task force of technical specialists simply does not work. It doesn't work because new thinking is required; a break with the past is imperative; and time is of the essence.

A final point on Phase III: I do not advise going through the process of evaluation and feedback as is done when implementing a transitional strategy. There is little time to undertake formal evaluation activity, and, while feedback and learning are important aspects of Systems Thinking, I prefer to use a much more informal, "quick and dirty" process. We learn by doing.

Bringing Transformational Change to a Close

I believe that an enterprise needs to transform itself only once during its life cycle. Organizations that continually porpoise or experience constant swings between extreme highs and extreme lows are not serving either their share owners or the stakeholders. Good managers, once they transform an enterprise, do not need to do it again if they adhere to the principles of continuous improvement and transitional change as outlined earlier in this chapter. An enterprise that is ahead of the curve and always anticipating, understanding, and taking action around the consequences of its choices and decisions does not experience the constant major shift in strategy required to achieve a fit with its environment.

HOW DO WE GET STARTED?

I get this question a lot. It is a great question and a useful test of whether one has thought through the real-life issues of making change in a large, complex enterprise. What I tell my clients is this: You can begin implementing the Governance Model with any of the loops included in the model. In some instances, the process of implementation may move with the bottom-up operations subsystem, the top-down strategy subsystem being examined simultaneously.

For example, Physicians Mutual began with the operations loop. The company spent considerable time making certain that business processes, including the potential consequences of those processes, were documented, operational, and producing targeted results. The firm then went on to implement the organization, management process, and information loop. In this case, the organization structure was redesigned and a system known as the Balanced Scorecard[1] was initiated. Finally, over a two-year period, the strategy and execution loops were implemented.

The point of the question "How do we get started?" first rests with the decision to implement the Governance Model and the System of Governance. That decided, the place to start is determined by the nature of the change to be undertaken. For transitional change as indicated with the Physicians Mutual case, beginning with the operations loop and moving around the Governance Model worked just fine. For transformational change, the strategy loop is usually the starting point. The message remains, "Get started."

CONCLUSION

I have often thought that I should place this chapter on Making It Happen as one of the earlier chapters in this book rather than the next to last chapter. By considering the strategies for change first, the reader might interpret the Governance Model and the ideas behind Systems Thinking with implementation in mind. I finally decided to leave the chapter where it is and put a note about reading it first in the Preface. I did this because most learning comes from the experiences garnered by taking the journey. I felt that the journey through this book was important and a prerequisite to deciding on which implementation strategy was appropriate.

Deciding how to make it happen is a Big Decision for the board and executive management. This decision cannot be delegated to anyone—consultants, senior management, or operating management. The board and executive management must own this decision and its consequences—risks.

The strategy for Making It Happen may be selected only after the decision to adopt the Governance Model as a framework for decision making has been made. Simply said, if we have not decided on a destination, any strategy will take us there. The Governance Model is the destination, and Making It Happen is the course by which we steer the ship to that destination.

NOTE

1. Robert S. Kaplan and David P. Norton, *The Balanced Scorecard* (Boston: Harvard Business School Press, 1996).

Where Do We Go from Here? Thoughts for the Board and Chief or C-Level Executives

INTRODUCTION

This book is being written in the fall–winter of 2002–2003 as one crisis in corporate governance after another surfaces. The SEC is busy with rules for the enforcement of Sarbanes-Oxley and the New York Stock Exchange and Nasdaq are drafting new regulations for their listed companies. State legislatures are desperately seeking new sources of revenue to close their budget gaps. The equity and debt markets are on a roller coaster. The Big Five accounting firms are now the Big Four. Lawyers themselves are being sued. We are fighting a war on terrorism and a war with Iraq. The environment loop has probably never produced as much "white water" as it is producing at present.

I am active on several nonprofit boards and one public company board. My colleagues on all of the boards raise the same questions or issues: "Where do we go from here?" People I talk to are asking, "Who would ever want to serve on the board of a public company?" Interestingly, as I recruit for my nonprofit boards, the first question from potential candidates has to do with liability insurance, rather than the mission or purpose of the organization.

Finally, as I conducted the research for this book through interviews with board members and other chief or "C-level" executives, I was constantly asked how many CEOs would permit their board members to participate in the Governance Model and System of Governance as I have depicted them." That is the toughest question of all. My answer, or at least the line of reasoning I put forward, is this:

■ Existing and potential board members will no longer permit their CEOs to keep them in the dark or underinformed. The idea of the CEO controlling the board is fast becoming a thing of the past.

■ CEOs are quickly concluding that their tenure is shrinking and that they must work with their boards whether they like it or not.

The convergence of these trends leads me to believe that boards will seek to be educated in how to do their jobs in a responsible way. Chief executive officers will also seek to be educated in how to work with their boards in ways that build trust and mutual respect.

I interviewed Ed Merino, CEO of Office of the Chairman, a consulting firm that specializes in corporate governance and board member education. Ed's principal messages to me were:

■ Board members and executives need a "highway system" or "rules of the road."
■ What makes a great board is trust, dialogue, and engaged debate.

It is my hope that the framework of the Governance Model will provide the "highway" in the form of a process for decision making and that the System of Governance and process of implementation will create the trust, dialogue, and engaged debate.

BIG DECISIONS

Many of the chapters of this book have brought to light what I call the Big Decisions, which relate to the choices available and the decisions made as a result of those choices. The Governance Model and the processes for implementing the System of Governance are based on anticipating, understanding, and taking action on the outcomes of choices and decisions—risks and rewards.

The choices and decisions described in the preceding chapters were enterprise-level decisions. The choices and decisions highlighted in this chapter are personal, not institutional. As I study the literature among professionals, executives, academics, and board members, and as I think about the individual roles of the members of the board and chief or C-level executives, the following Big Decisions continuously surface.

■ An acceptance of individual responsibility for the outcomes of choices and decisions of the Extended Enterprise.
■ An explicit requirement for information and education.
■ A commitment to doing the work required to be knowledgeable and effective.

- A commitment to the long-term survival and growth of the enterprise.
- A commitment to ethical, not just legal behavior.

To me, these decisions on the part of everyone in the Extended Enterprise form the basis for the culture of the organization. These decisions and commitments start with each individual who serves on the board of directors and each chief or C-level executive who steers the organization on its course.

IT ALL STARTS WITH THE BOARD

First, not a single person I interviewed even remotely suggested that board members should become involved in execution or operations in order to fulfill their duties as directors. No one is suggesting that the board second-guess management except for the provision of Sarbanes-Oxley that permits boards to hire their own advisors. Rather, the boards need information. This is one of the reasons why the Governance Model has a subsystem for dealing with information.

Information and Education

During the interview with Gerry Rosenfeld, which I cited earlier, we discussed this issue of information. Gerry used the phrase, "asymmetric skewing of information in favor of management." This imbalance of information, particularly around outcomes of the Big Decisions that relate to strategy, should not be tolerated by the board. I understand the issue that many large organizations are viewed as too complex for the board to comprehend. That complexity is a reality that may be dealt with only through education and information. Boards may begin this process of education and information by applying the concepts of Systems Thinking to the choices and decisions at a strategy level. The boards must play out the potential consequences of those choices and decisions in ways that identify risks and rewards and establish metrics for monitoring and tracking feedback and learning. On the subject of education, board members will have to become more knowledgeable about the enterprises over which they exercise stewardship.

In my view, board members do not need to be industry experts, but they should be quick studies around the big issues and major decisions of the industries in which their organizations compete. The reasons why I do not think deep industry expertise is a prerequisite include:

■ Management has, or should have, such competencies, and board members will never have as much industry and company experience and expertise as those executives who live there every day.

■ A board dominated by industry players, including those members of management who are on the board, is subject to seeing issues and decisions the way everyone in the industry sees them.

■ Boards require diverse points of view from industries that tend to go through the same cycles, and functional expertise, particularly in strategy and finance, to provide diversity in the makeup of the board itself.

Education is a prerequisite for good governance. Decision making requires information, knowledge, and judgment. These characteristics require education and technical skills. I have had a number of recent experiences in which I have been asked to facilitate annual board retreats for the express purpose of establishing a dialogue among board members and executive management on the subjects of strategy and decision making. In many situations, I am also joined by an investment banker who may provide the institutional investor and hopefully the ultimate share owner perspective.

When discussing the issues of education on the subject of governance and board responsibilities, it is important to emphasize the working relationship between the board and management. If mutual respect and trust do not characterize that relationship, compliance around such issues as competency, independence, and ethical behavior will not assure the survivability and growth of the enterprise. Decision making is first of all about openness and candor—all of the voices must be heard. Openness and candor will not be present without mutual respect and trust.

How Much Time Should Be Required of Board Members?

The quick answer is, "a lot." Board members, even in companies that are not particularly complex, need to spend a lot of time getting to know the people, culture, and decision-making processes of the enterprise. In the language of Systems Thinking, they must understand the Governance Model and the System of Governance even though the processes will not carry those terms. In my view, a board that is really active only when a transaction of some sort is being contemplated will not have the context in which to anticipate and understand the consequences of such transactions.

Finally, to answer the question about how much time is required: I think that for most moderately complex corporations, a board member should spend a minimum of a day a week, on average, on board business of one kind or another. That time may include:

- Board meetings
- Education and training
- Marketing events
- Site visits
- Customer calls
- Committee meetings
- Due diligence
- Special projects
- Strategic planning

Four hundred hours a year sounds like a lot, and it is. However, I believe that those hours have to be invested so that when the Big Decisions arrive, the entire board is prepared. Board members and board candidates must decide if they are willing to make the commitment of time and energy to the service of the enterprise.

Why Should Anyone Want to Serve on a Public Company Board?

This spoken and unspoken question is at the top of the mind of every director I interviewed. With all of the public scrutiny, paperwork hassles, financial liability, risk of reputation, and time requirements, the question of why is paramount. Not surprisingly, the answer I received from nearly every interview was, "To make a difference." I received this answer from directors who serve on both for-profit and not-for-profit boards. In today's world, no one is sitting on any board for the prestige, power, or money. There is simply not enough of any of these so-called rewards to justify the risks involved.

The idea of making a difference would have been expected from prospective not-for-profit board members. Most not-for-profits are mission-driven, and therefore board members self-select in order to help achieve the mission and to make a difference in the lives of those touched by the organization. Making a difference is the driver or motivation behind the board members of the for-profit companies as well. Most directors wish to make a difference, not by working as individuals who advise executives, but as members of a team made up of like-minded leaders who love the collaboration, dialogue, and problem solving inherent in their role. It is through the exchange of experience, knowledge, and values that board members make a difference. Great enterprises are characterized as having exceptional leaders, and those leaders are put in place by exceptional boards.

How Should Conflicts Be Handled?

Experts in conflict resolution tell me that there are three ways to handle conflict:

1. Ignore the conflict and hope that it will be resolved on its own.
2. Apply power and resolve the conflict by dint of position and authority or personality.
3. Establish a dialogue around the issue in order that the multiple perspectives may be considered.

The Governance Model and the System of Governance provide the framework and the process for the third option. In the presence of mutual respect and trust, the Big Decisions, including the consequences of those decisions, are worked out through collaboration and dialogue between the board and executive management for the benefit of the share owners and stakeholders.

In those situations in which, for whatever reasons, dialogue doesn't work, the board acting on its own must rise to the occasion. The board is an agent for the owners, not for management. When problems and conflicts with management cannot be resolved, the board makes a major decision to replace management. That is all there is to it. Board members who are not prepared for CEO succession planning are not doing their jobs.

THE SHIP AS A METAPHOR FOR THE ENTERPRISE

Some consultants and writers use sports metaphors to illustrate teamwork and leadership. If sports examples make the point, that is great. In this chapter on personal choices, roles, and responsibilities, I have chosen a nautical metaphor because the so-called management structure of an enterprise, the vessel, must successfully interface with the environment, the sea, if the objectives of the enterprise are to be achieved. The leadership and management structure of the sea has worked for thousands of years, and in many ways provides great examples of personal responsibility and the requirement for collaboration. In some cases, my metaphor is stretched a bit, but I hope my points are nevertheless, communicated. My use of a ship and the sea as a metaphor for the enterprise and its environment is not intended to portray Captain Bligh as a hero or to illustrate the leadership of a Shackleton, but rather to evoke the management skills required for a successful ocean voyage.

The CEO as Captain Steers the Course

A sailing vessel has one skipper. The tradition of the sea, brought about by the need for the vessel to continuously cope with its ever-changing environment, requires that one person be accountable for the ship and its crew. There is complete clarity on this point among the members of the board, who represent the owners and the officers and members of the crew.

A good skipper constantly seeks input from his or her crew, trusts the advice of the officers, and communicates effectively to all stakeholders. A poor skipper does not last long. The stakes of survival are too great. The point of this metaphor is clear. The accountability for the success of the voyage rests directly on the shoulders of the captain; it cannot be delegated. So, too, in my opinion, is the accountability for the survival and growth of the enterprise. Responsibility may be delegated to the officers and crew, but in the final analysis it is the CEO who is accountable. This is an issue of clarity, not power.

The COO as First Mate or Executive Officer

The role of the chief operating officer is well established in management practice. The COO carries out the decisions of the board and CEO just as the first mate or executive officer is number two in the hierarchy of the vessel. Generally, the COO is in training to become a CEO. The CEO, however, cannot delegate the accountability for the growth and survival of the enterprise. The COO or first mate does not set or steer the course independent of the CEO or captain.

The COO, working with the CFO, CIO, and CRO, may well focus on execution within the Extended Enterprise while the captain deals more with the external environment. It is the job of the COO to manage the details. In any event, all chief or C-level executives, together with the board, collaborate to implement the Governance Model and the System of Governance. It is this policy-level team, referred to earlier as the policy committee, that creates the environment for improved decision making based on feedback and learning. In many ways, the COO, as the first mate, provides much of the energy and spark required for the policy committee to work well together.

The CFO as Navigator

Again, referring back to the Governance Model, I see the chief financial officer as having direct oversight of the organization, management process, and information subsystem. The CFO may collaborate with other chief or C-level executives, such as the chief operating officer, the chief risk officer, and the chief information officer, who may oversee certain elements of the subsystem. It is the CFO who, according to most corporate bylaws and security regulations, has the personal responsibility for the accuracy and compliance of financial information and results.

The CFO, to continue my metaphor of a ship and the sea, is responsible for processing and portraying all of the information required to know where we have been, where we are, and where we are going. The lives of the crew and the safety of the vessel depend on the skill and integrity of the navigator.

In addition to adopting the personal Big Decisions outlined earlier in this chapter, the CFO must be relied on by the CEO to present a factual and unbiased view of the Extended Enterprise and where it stands in relation to its environment. The CFO must be able to present or represent several perspectives of the enterprise at the same time and do so in a way that is balanced in its presentation. For example, the CFO of an insurance company must present an actuarial, statutory, and GAAP (generally accepted accounting principles) perspective recognizing that each has a different purpose and audience, but all must be internally consistent.

The CFO must present favorable outcomes and prospects with the same balance and integrity as unfavorable results and projections are presented. If necessary, the CFO must stand alone and risk being blamed as the messenger in carrying out his or her responsibility to present the unfavorable consequences of decisions. The board and the rest of the enterprise depend on the CFO to tell it like it is.

In my most recent experience in helping to implement the Governance Model, it is the CFO who takes overall responsibility for managing the process. In most instances, the CFO is the keeper of the financial database from which much information is derived as well as the linkages to the operating systems that provide the necessary metrics for measuring feedback. The CFO also has the competencies that ensure the integrity and reliability of the information used for decision-making purposes.

CFOs and navigators have a lot in common. When the ship arrives safely at its destination or the organization achieves its objectives, all expectations are met and little notice is given to the day-to-day taking of sights and plotting of course corrections. The CFO and the navigator get little credit when all goes as planned. But when the vessel is off course or goals are missed . . .

The CIO as the Keeper of the Systems and Data

I may be stretching the nautical metaphor a bit, but all of the measuring devices, gauges, instruments, and data aboard a modern ship must be integrated and working reliably. The financial and other metrics used by the captain, navigator, engineer, and operating personnel must be held together and present an integrated and consistent view of what is happening as well as the status of the measuring systems themselves. Our Extended Enterprise simply will no longer function without information and the integration of that information. It is the chief information officer who provides the raw materials, data, and permits the conversion of that data into the information that provides the required feedback and enables learning to occur.

The Governance Model will not work without technology and data. The CIO enables the Governance Model to work because he or she brings to the enterprise the competencies required to capture and process information from strategy through execution to operations and the organization, management process, and information subsystems.

In the connected world of cause and effect, feedback and learning, it is the CIO who puts the technology-enabling processes in place in the form of data, communications, computing, and software necessary to anticipate, understand, and take action around the consequences of choices and decisions.

The CRO as the Tactician

The tactician on an ocean voyage employs Systems Thinking as he or she anticipates, understands, and takes action around the decisions made by the board and the CEO. The chief risk officer is the officer who applies Systems Thinking to the Extended Enterprise.

The nautical metaphor may be once again a bit stretched, but my vision of the CRO is that of monitoring and tracking of outcomes as well as processing the threats and opportunities emerging from all facets of the Extended Enterprise and its environment. The CRO is the eyes and ears of the CEO using information processed by the CIO and applied by the CFO.

I was quite skeptical of the need for the position that has emerged as chief risk officer. It seemed to me that the CRO was going to begin by assessing risks and putting in place all kinds of expensive bureaucratic processes for dealing with outcomes. As I have reiterated many times in this book, I don't believe that one can manage outcomes or risks, but rather the process must deal with the decisions that produce consequences. Therefore, if the role of the CRO as it was to emerge was to go down the path of conventional wisdom, I would not be in favor of such a position.

However, as the Governance Model took form, it occurred to me that the role of the CRO might add value if that role were to track the consequences of Big Decisions within the Extended Enterprise and monitor threats from the external environment. The role of the CRO as the implementer of Systems Thinking throughout the Extended Enterprise could be very effective and useful. This role as I envision it really adds value only in the context of a changed perspective about risk itself. Otherwise, the role will create work that may be performed just as effectively within the silos of the organization.

Who Is the CRO?　　Most of our chief or C-level executives, including the CIO, have now been around awhile and have become part of the management body of knowledge. The CRO of course is a new role, the scope of which is just now emerging. I have met a number of CROs who are very mathematically inclined and believe that everything can be quantified and measured. The very act of quantifying what I believe to be largely unquantifiable to me misses the point. Certainly, some potential losses such as tangible assets may be quantified in terms of replacement value or economic loss, but, for the most part, it is very difficult to quantify the losses of the more intangible assets. Further, attempts to measure the outcomes of Big Decisions to follow or not to follow a course of action are largely impossible. While good analytic skills are important on the part of the CRO, they are not sufficient to serve as integrators of the Governance Model.

The CRO, from my perspective, must first be a systems thinker, that is, a person who is technically grounded in General Systems Theory and is able to apply Systems Thinking to the subject of governance and risk. The CRO must be able to communicate with the governance committee of the board as well as be capable of tracking potential and actual consequences of decisions throughout the Extended Enterprise. The CRO must also be able to anticipate, understand, and recommend action arising from events throughout the Extended Enterprise and its environment.

CONCLUSION

The days of the imperial CEO and the uninvolved board are gone. One only has to look at the environment loop to see the impact of social forces on public policy, combined with the impact of competition and capital markets, to grasp the white-water convergence on the enterprise loop.

Boards and their governance committees on the one hand, and chief or C-level executives who have always been responsible stewards of the firm's assets on the other hand, will combine to regain the confidence of the investing public.

Boards and chief or C-level executives will once again come to realize that their goals and the goals of their share owners and stakeholders are aligned. The growth and survival of the enterprise over the long run creates share owner value, not a short-term focus on stock prices. Stock prices, like risks and rewards, are outcomes of sound decisions—governance—over the long run. Boards and chief or C-level executives who focus on feedback and learning and the consequences of their decisions will provide the Tone at the Top required of great enterprises.

Afterword

The future of any organization can be traced to the consequences of decisions—those well made, poorly made, and not made at all. All decisions are multidimensional in terms of time. What, where, and when are the risks? Who is responsible for identifying, calculating, and monitoring risks?

Risks, of course, are of several types and carry varying consequences. In his writing, Jack Shaw seeks to link decisions and their inherent risks with the responsibilities of governance. His notion is that in this rapidly changing world, boards and senior executives need better tools to anticipate and proactively address the risks associated with decisions.

Shaw brings a fresh view to risk management, owing to a lifetime of experience consulting with many leading companies, as well as to his long personal association with Peter Drucker, the acknowledged authority on organizations and their behavior.

We at Edward Jones welcome this new approach to a subject that from time to time keeps every senior manager and board member awake at night. As somewhat of an endangered species—we are the last significant partnership remaining in the securities industry—our interest in the management of risk is more than casual.

In our organization, the identification and assessment of risk is not the job of top management. It is a job shared by all associates. Ultimately, though, it ends up at the doorstep of our management committee. We view risk and decision making in terms of a diverse, sometimes fragmented model.

We begin by identifying, reviewing, and weighing external risks. In most of these areas, we exert little control and are looking at risks that can extend well into the future. Examples include:

- The economy.
- The market.
- Changes in law and regulation.
- Competitors' behavior.

At the next level, there are risks associated with several elements of our basic strategy. Here we have more control; however, we can still face a long time horizon. Among these factors are:

197

- Our business model.
- Our emphasis on serving one customer.
- Our trade-offs (that is, what we choose not to do).
- Our form of organization, which is a partnership.
- Affordability.

The operation and administration of our business creates another set of risks. They are frequently more immediate in nature, but not always. Some have long tails:

- The products we offer.
- Our sales literature and training.
- Our reliance on technology.
- Our compliance function.

Interday activities introduce yet another set of risks, and these are immediate:

- Carrying product inventory.
- Potential errors, which require strictly enforced policies.
- Processing transactions and collecting funds.

In spite of this sober recital of risk and the pain it can cause, one must remember that without risk, there can be no reward.

To address and mitigate risk, leadership must be able to turn to a set of five tools:

1. The organization's culture and values.
2. Systems.
3. Training.
4. Able management.
5. Fresh eyes. In our case, these are the external members of our compliance and investment policy committees.

The most important role in corporate governance may well be that of recognizing and monitoring the seductive nature of risk. In any competitive area, there are only a few ways to increase profitability. One is to establish a sustainable competitive advantage. Another is to become more efficient. The third, which often happens unconsciously, is to take greater risks. Risk, after all, isn't risky until one is injured or ruined by it.

To the extent that Jack Shaw heightens managers' and directors' consciousness about the importance of risk, his work can only make organizations and their leaders more effective. We thank him for devoting himself to this important work and for sharing his insights with us.

—JOHN W. BACHMANN
Managing Partner, Edward Jones

One ship drives east and another drives west
With the selfsame winds that blow.
'Tis the set of sails and not the gales
Which tells us the way to go.

—"Winds of Fate," Ella Wheeler Wilcox,
Poet and Journalist, 1850–1919

Index

that those strategic and execution decisions are reexamined. Operations management, if it is doing its job within the Governance Model, has the direct responsibility for providing such feedback.

An Example I worked with one multibillion-dollar service company that embarked on a series of successful, relatively small acquisitions in related fields. The due diligence process worked quite well throughout the Governance Model. A potential acquisition surfaced that would double the size of the company and make it number one in size within its industry sector. The decision-making process, which was really a due diligence process, moved from the board of directors through executive and senior management with the conclusion that the acquisition was "a stretch, but doable." As the decision moved to operations management, the unintended consequences began to surface. Operations management, in examining the details of integration, concluded that as a result of the size, complexity, and culture of the operations of the potential acquisition, "We would end up looking like them." That conclusion was devastating. It was also true. The successful acquiring company would have been so diluted by the relatively unsuccessful acquisition that the character of the acquiring company would be lost. The conclusion was fed back to executive management and the board with the result that the acquisition was abandoned. A decision *not to do* something is often more important than a decision *to do* something. Operations management had fulfilled its responsibilities. The board, executive management, and senior management had fulfilled their accountabilities. The Governance Model and the System of Governance had performed their functions.

Management Process

I briefly touched on management process in the preceding chapters on the Governance Model. This discussion focused not on process for the sake of process or control but on processes related to decision making. Strategy dealt with those processes for handling the future unknowns, and execution dealt with the knowable outcomes, while operations dealt with the known results. This section on management process carries forward the ideas around decision making at the strategy, execution, and operations levels to the continuous processes required to track performance compared to plans developed at those three levels. The continuous monitoring of actual performance and the decisions required to stay on track are at least as important an aspect of the Governance Model as the annual planning cycle. In fact, it is the continuous monitoring of cause and effect that enables feedback and learning to take place. Systems Thinking is a daily, minute-by-minute perspective across the Extended Enterprise.